Circle of Grace

Circle of Grace

A True Story of Extraordinary Faith
and the Power of Prayer

Mikie Casem

AuthorHouse™
1663 Liberty Drive
Bloomington, IN 47403
www.authorhouse.com
Phone: 1-800-839-8640

Published by AuthorHouse   05/22/2013

ISBN: 978-1-4817-5167-4 (sc)
ISBN: 978-1-4817-5163-6 (hc)
ISBN: 978-1-4817-5166-7 (e)

Library of Congress Control Number: 2013908478

Acknowledgements

Theresa Palumbo, without you there is no story. Thanks for allowing me to tell our story and for personally sharing your own experiences during our journey in this book. No amount of words can ever describe our love for you and your family.

Rita, in the best of times and the worst of times, for half a century, you have been at my side: my bride, chauffer and caregiver. Your patience and unselfishness have been my anchors. Your pragmatic spirit has kept us moving forward all these years. Thanks for keeping me focused in telling our story and helping me re-connect the dots of our remarkable journey.

Thanks to our Friday Night Gang, Smoke (the cat), and especially Jimmy and Dottie Dunham for hosting our traditional, weekly, backyard gathering all these years; for your camaraderie; for our shared good, home cooking, laughter, and a few tears around the cozy fire; and for your hearty encouragement to write this book.

Debbie Audilet, my Editor, thanks so much for generously saying yes to this project and managing to include it in your busy life as wife, mother of four children, college instructor and volunteer at St. Paul Catholic School. Your diligent assistance has been invaluable in making this book a reality.

To Personal Caregivers

The unsung heroes who clutch appointment schedules, water bottles and cloth sacks jammed with meds, test kits, crackers and cell phones and travel alongside their loved ones on the crowded path to hope.

"I was a stranger and you welcomed me . . .
ill and you cared for me."

(Matthew 25:35-36)

PROLOGUE

A Time to Mourn and a Time to Dance

As Catholic Christians, no one ever said this business of following in Jesus' footsteps to get to heaven would be a walk in the park. Despite life's numerous blessings, our path is mined with Satan's scrumptious temptations, physical afflictions and increasing civil scorn for traditional moral values. The daily choices we make or do not make certainly affect our journey. Stepping into a self-inflicted pot hole, getting blindsided by one of life's sucker punches or finding ourselves tangled up in somebody else's mess can send us reeling or put us flat on our face. Pushing on up the path can be a grueling challenge, often to the breaking point and beyond. Somehow finding the strength to simply survive can become a horrific nightmare. Regardless of our situation, up the path ahead of us in His human form, Christ, the Son of God looked up to His Heavenly Father for that strength as He completed His own journey and set the course for ours by dragging His bloody cross and pushing on up the hill to Calvary to save us.

Today's social norms disdain patience, inconvenience, commitment and the slightest hint of discomfort. We are bombarded with the notion that we can control or find just about everything ourselves. However, no GPS navigation system can plot the unpredictable twists and turns of life or the unimaginable impact that our faith can have on the outcome. We do, however, have a pretty remarkable roadmap to guide us on our journey. It has been around a while, and it is closer than one would think. I didn't really discover it until my life almost ended.

If you are like me, familiar scriptural readings and gospels we have heard a zillion times tend to roll by like the drone of rush hour traffic outside. Whether we are trying to pick up the pieces or simply catch our breath, perhaps we will recall that through the words of these inspired sacred scripture writers, God is speaking to each of us. If we listen a bit more attentively, or better yet, allow our self to take even a few minutes to re-visit daily scripture readings, we just might find in many of these verses Our Creator has woven a remarkable roadmap for our trip, complete with blinking lights, stop signs and rest areas. For example, God describes the long haul and puts the ups and downs of our journey in perspective. He reminds us there is a rhythm to life with each cycle having its own challenges and gifts. Seasonal changes bring a waxing and waning of nature, just as our spiritual life has periods of growth and stagnation, light and darkness. "There is an appointed time for everything . . . a time to be born and a time to die, a time to plant and a time to uproot, a time to kill and a time to heal, a time to mourn and a time to dance, a time to embrace and a time not to embrace, a time to seek and a time to lose, a time to be silent, and a time to speak . . . God has made everything appropriate to its time" (Ecclesiastes 3: 1-11). How often when we're preparing for a trip do we find ourselves jamming our suitcase full of stuff, just in case we might need it, only to regret having brought it and lugged it around, distracting us from enjoying the present? Jesus cautions His apostles to travel lightly on their journey. "Take nothing for the journey; neither walking stick, nor sack, nor food, nor money and let no one take a second tunic" (Luke 9:3). Jesus' advice can also apply on a deeper level. How often do we cling to certain past experiences, hurts, regrets and fears that wind up bogging us down and inhibiting our journey? Beginning with His first miracle at the wedding feast at Cana until His final breath on the cross, Jesus' ministry was all about spiritual and physical healing of folks in need around Him, familiar faces, strangers and enemies. Is it just a coincidence that in most cases Jesus' acts of healing involved someone bringing the afflicted people or their need to Him? As the Son of God, Jesus reminds us that we are made in His image and likeness; how we treat one another is how we treat Him, and He minces no words in reminding us that we are to serve one another. "Whatever you did for the least one of these brothers of mine, you did to me" (Matthew 25:40). At the Last Supper, He demonstrated this point of serving one another by washing the feet of the apostles. When Peter resisted, Jesus rebuked him and warned about being too stiff necked to receive needed help from someone else, "Unless I wash you, you will have no inheritance with me" (John 13:8). Through our actions, God provides His love, strength and hope, His grace to anyone in need. Reaching out to another person often involves more than our time and material things. It can mean giving away our comfort zone, privacy, peace of mind and more. Our gift of free will allows us to make that choice. I have found a reasonable gauge for where I am on my own journey of faith. It lies in my response to a question I frequently ask myself: how open am I to seek and share God's grace each day?

It is easy to miss the point, thinking grace has to be associated with some great epiphany. Simply through prayer and the Sacraments, we can strive to invoke God's grace upon ourselves, but the business of everyday life has a way of masking the many opportunities we have to share or receive grace. Some of these moments arrive like an invisible breeze wafting through an open window in the form of a warm smile or an encouraging handshake. Others come at us out of nowhere, like demanding, warp-speed decisions to bite our tongue at the maniac who just cut us off on the freeway. We can also be dusted with grace simply by being inspired by the way someone lives his/her life. Grace can even come without us being aware, like someone praying for us or putting in a good word on our behalf. God describes these transparent moments in the Old Testament. "I will be like the dew to Israel" (Hosea 14:5). An opportunity for grace can be as close as a family member or as far away as a tiny voice beckoning us from halfway around the world. We never know how our response to grace will change someone's life—or our own—forever.

In his writings, C.S. Lewis hits the mark when he says a lot of us sincere Christians perform good acts with an underlying confidence that we will all add up, somehow impress God and ultimately earn us a place in heaven. Lewis points out that this is a misguided focus because true believers understand that no amount of good acts can earn us heaven. They realize that if we are repentant of our sins, through His death and resurrection, Christ has already saved us. Lewis concludes by reminding us that the reality of our Christian faith is that the only reason we perform good acts is because we are motivated to reflect Christ's life within us.

At times, each of us has encountered an instance when the grace we seek to impart on someone else finds its way back to us. Typically, we slough off such occurrences as a turn of good fortune or what goes around comes around. I did too, until our phone rang that afternoon in early February 2011. So many people had been praying for me, but my end-stage illness had continued to sap my energy level, and I could feel things slipping away. My wife Rita answered the phone and handed it to me with a smile. A familiar voice offered help; she offered grace. Suddenly, I was gripped with the unmistakable feeling that something pretty wonderful was about to happen. God was unfolding a miracle. My life was about to be saved! The words Circle of Grace flashed through my mind. We were experiencing God's Circle of Grace.

This book unfolds a unique story of how the lives of two persons intersected not once, but twice. At each encounter, one individual found the other in the midst of an agonizing crisis and offered the other a whole new lease on life. This story shares the journey that led us to this Circle of Grace. Our journey actually began nearly fifty years ago when Rita first met (well, actually found) me hiding from her in a rather wacky place. Now, I've realized that daring to retrace my footsteps half a century or so to share this story was a daunting and imperfect endeavor: a risky task, eliciting a kaleidoscope of emotions. Early on, I was struck by the countless opportunities I have had to share or receive grace. Just as quickly, I painfully noticed how often I deflected most of these encounters with my veneer of complacency or an air of self-righteousness. Peeking into the rear view mirror, it was hard not to miss the endless parade of predicaments I had gotten into and somehow out of over a lifetime. For me, this was proof enough that despite our clumsiness and failings, just as He did with Peter, Christ never gives up on us. He continues to demonstrate His mercy by sending many holy, sometimes perhaps not so holy, and even a few bothersome people our way; each in his/her own manner help us inch ourselves along life's path. Scores of caring folks have propped me up or patiently nudged me toward my ultimate goal of heaven. This includes the guidance and genuine friendship of many Catholic Clergy and Religious. There are many individuals who have helped me that I have never met, but that's okay. God knows them each by name.

This is a true story of hope and the power of prayer. This story shares the experiences of two ordinary people who had the faith to offer one another an extraordinary gift of kindness and the unimaginable gift God revealed to each of them.

CONTENTS

Chapter 1

The Three R's and Steel-Toed Boots

Friday, November 20, 1942 found an unusual heat wave sweeping the east coast. I remember Mom telling me temperatures were pushing eighty that day when I was born at Washington, DC's old Garfield Hospital. She also recounted the concern she and Dad had about the kidney disorder I was suffering from and said that was the day she first started praying to St. Jude, Patron of Hopeless Cases. Msgr. James Smythe, Pastor at Shrine of the Sacred Heart Catholic Church, sprinkled me with my first official doses of grace in the Sacrament of Baptism, and I was anointed Maurice Patrick Casem. Shortly afterward, I was rushed to Children's Hospital where tests revealed one of my kidneys appeared to be doing most of the work. My persistent lethargic behavior and high temperature brought concerns that perhaps the Angel of Death was hovering nearby. Msgr. Smythe was summoned again, promptly dispensing another round of grace by conferring "Extreme Unction" (Sacrament of the Sick). I made a surprisingly quick recovery, and my parents were allowed to bring me home. During the next several years, I was a frequent visitor to Children's Hospital with raging urinary tract infections. Over time, these flare ups subsided in frequency and intensity but never completely went away. It was during one of those early stays as an infant at Children's Hospital when the nurses suggested to my parents that I definitely reminded them of a "Mikie." My folks took a liking to my new moniker, and it has been Mikie ever since.

Despite scrunching down at my desk, intently drawing a sailboat on the inside back cover of my blue Baltimore Catechism, Sister Hilary, our second grade teacher at Sacred Heart School, had her sights on me. A tug on my ear startled me from my masterpiece. It was, of course, Sister who just a minute ago was up front extolling the virtues of our upcoming Sacraments of First Confession and First Communion. This short, be-speckled, Dominican nun had an uncanny manner of reining in the attention of her rambunctious audience of seven-year-olds. Whatever it took, she was equally adept at bopping a blackboard eraser off the top of our heads at twenty feet or silently creeping up behind us. However, Sister also managed to diffuse my particular trepidation over my stage debut as Dopey in our upcoming second grade class play, *Snow White and the Seven Dwarfs*. Her comforting words assured me that, no, I did not have to wear a silly pair of pointed ears because my own ears were big enough and would do just fine. When the bell rang and we marched single file out of class, we knew Sister liked us because she usually patted everyone on top of the head. Her latest words of wisdom stuck with me, for a little while at least. Her simple definition of grace is still etched in my noggin, "Grace is being nice to each other every day."

A litany of other Dominican and later Benedictine nuns at St. Anthony's labored over me during elementary school. For over a century, dedicated religious women such as these infused generations of young people in the rigors of the three R's and strove to show us how wonderfully our moral compasses aligned with the principles and tenets of the Catholic Church. Sadly, today nuns have all but disappeared from the classroom. Thanks to my parents' financial sacrifices, my siblings, Tommy and Patty, and I were able to continue our Catholic education past grammar school. It took me five years at Gonzaga High School, but eventually, a host of Jesuits like Fr. Hocking S.J. and Fr. Hammett S.J. got their point across about accountability. At the same time, they managed to convince me what end of a Bunsen burner to light and that all of Gaul was divided into three parts (or was it four?). At Wheeling College (now Wheeling Jesuit University), Fr. Jim O'Brien S.J. (O.B.) shared with our Theology class the insight of St. Ignatius that leadership starts with being a good servant. O.B. cautioned us that the call to serve others is rarely a planned event and typically arrives at the most inconvenient time. Before year's end, O.B.'s words sprung to life late one evening during a driving March rainstorm. Downing the last few drops in our mugs at *Moxie's* pub, my cohorts Pete Daley, Mal Luebkert and I clamored out the front door to join scores of other Wheeling students wading from house to house in the pitch black, helping our stranded, frightened neighbors from a springtime flood that had turned the Ohio River and our neighboring creek into a raging, frigid monster.

During college, I spent the sweltering DC summers working as a general laborer for a large commercial construction contractor. Our job sites included places like RFK Stadium and the Sam Rayburn Congressional Office building on Capitol Hill. It was a baptism into real life, an unexpected education not found in any textbook. Classrooms were outdoor arenas enveloped in clouds of dust and a symphony of deafening noises where beer bellied men bent over jackhammers and enormous pile drivers relentlessly pounded steel pilings into the earth with an agonizing cadence. Crane engines whirled while operators skillfully swung their towering booms laden with weighty cargo toward groups of men barking orders from the edge of nearby scaffolds. I was a boy among brawny men twice my age who performed this backbreaking and often dangerous work for a living. Steel-toed boots and hard hats are worn for a reason. Taunting came with the job. As a neophyte learning how to walk across an I-beam five stories up or struggling to push a wheelbarrow load of concrete, I was an easy target. However, the boisterous chiding never masked the watchful eye my gruff co-workers kept over me. Over time, many of these foreboding strangers invited me into their world, whether that meant joining them in a few rounds of gin rummy at lunchtime or passing the bottle around after work on a Friday. During my last few days on the job, I found myself pondering the previous four summers. I had escaped several close calls with only a broken finger and a lacerated leg. I had managed to save a good amount of money toward school, but I could not shake the memory of seeing the fellow next to me lose half of his hand when a cable suddenly snapped or hearing the ungodly scream of a man falling to his death. For the first time, I witnessed the frailty of life and learned that survival often comes down to strangers looking out for one another. Earthy colleagues like James Taylor and Football Brown ushered this skinny, white kid into manhood. As I walked away from the job that last day, a handful of men came up to me, extended a calloused hand into mine and nodded silently. One or two folks minced words cautioning me not to screw up an opportunity they never had—a chance to earn a college degree.

Chapter 2

Keep the Faith

My Dad, Maurice Joseph (Maury) Casem, was a strapping six-foot, second generation Irishman who parted his coal black hair in the middle. I called him Pop. He was born in Wilkes-Barre, PA. His father left home when Pop was young, leaving his mother to raise four sons alone. As the oldest boy, Pop helped shoulder his mother's burden and began working at a very early age. His education ended with high school, so he knew well the value of an education and never let any of us three kids forget it. Pop was old school, shot and a beer, and no gimmies. Starting as a foot patrolman with the Washington, DC Metropolitan Police Department, he worked his way up to precinct detective, earning nine commendations along the way. His joys were simple and few, fussing over a handful of his favorite flowers, gardenias, in our tiny yard and later cooling off on the front porch with a couple of cold Carlings and a few smokes. It was not unusual on his day off for Pop and a few of his police cronies to enjoy each other's company gathered around our smoke filled dining room table to play a few hands of gin. Trying to make ends meet on a cop's salary for his family of five, while also helping with college tuitions for my brother Tommy and me, Pop had no problem spending a Saturday afternoon trying to get lucky at the track. Unfortunately, the years of dealing with homicides, rapes and robberies took a sad toll on Pop and our family life. Coming through the front door after work with the smiling face of dad, after having spent the past ten hours wrestling with a group of thugs, didn't always work. That is just the way it was. Thankfully, Pop knew the value of our Catholic faith. He did what he could to keep us in Catholic schools, and while he may have not always been there, he made sure the rest of us attended Sunday Mass. My Mom, Margaret (Maggie) Young Casem, was a diminutive, salt and pepper haired woman, second oldest of eight siblings, from Lancaster, PA. She dutifully managed to always have us three kids neatly dressed while keeping us in tow with her firm look and an even firmer faith. Like my father, Mom enjoyed her Herbert Tareyton cigarettes, but unlike Pop, she preferred her beer room temperature, a trait she attributed to her German ancestry.

I was home from my junior year in college working my summer construction job when without warning, life flipped upside down and came to a sorrowful numbing stop. Getting dressed for the day shift one hot July morning, Pop suffered a major heart attack and was rushed to the hospital. That evening, when the family was finally admitted to visit him in ICU, it was quite a shock seeing Pop hooked to a tangle of tubes tethered to blinking and beeping machines. None of us had ever seen our father, this tough Irish cop, look so vulnerable. Pop slowly opened his eyes and attempted to speak, but nothing came out. Mom was already nervously fingering her rosary, and nobody knew what to say. Finally, my older brother Tommy blurted out, "Will the insurance cover this?" Pop weakly waved him off and mumbled, "That's not important now." After a few minutes of awkward small talk, the nurse stuck her head into the room and whispered it was time for Pop to get some rest. One by one, we shuffled to his bedside. Looking down at him, I was hoping Pop wouldn't notice my eyes glistening. I clumsily extended my hand into his cold palm and was surprised by the strength of his grip. He managed to look up at me in an almost apologetic stare and, in an unusual whisper, mouthed his familiar, stoic refrain, "Keep the faith." The next day, July 25, 1963, at the age of fifty-three, Pop passed away.

I was twenty years old when Pop died. Mom's health had already begun to deteriorate, and now she became more nervous than usual. My younger sister, Patty, had recently married Billy Elliott, a friend of Tommy's who had finished his third year at Georgetown and was living at home. Pop's sudden passing left each of us kids with the stark reality that now we were grownups, and we were the ones who would have to look after our Mom and help her shoulder her new life as a widow in the family homestead: a modest, tan brick duplex home at 1013 Upshur Street in the tree-lined Michigan Park neighborhood in the outer, northeast section of Washington.

Almost four months to the day following Pop's passing, President Kennedy was assassinated in November. I was in my junior year at Wheeling, and because of the national tragedy, classes had been suspended. I decided to do the usual and hitch-hike the three hundred miles home from Wheeling, WV, this time to see about a blind date my friend Dave Holden had been badgering me about. I was not into blind dates, especially when Dave was involved. Like me, he was a prankster, and Dave's description of this girl with a "sweet personality" sent shivers through me. I had visions of being introduced to a large German Shepherd or worse, but he insisted this Rita was for real. Dave and Rita were senior classmates at nearby St. Anthony's High School, located in the historic Brookland area of northeast DC, once my pre-dawn *Washington Post* paper route, a short distance from Turkey Thicket playground, the Franciscan Monastery and Catholic University. I convinced Dave that before going out with this Rita, I wanted to see her without her seeing me. Dave countered, "Okay, how about if you just hear her?" That is when we came up with the nit-wit scheme for me to hide in the trunk of Dave's '49 Ford coupe while he drove to pick her up at school. I could at least hear if she sounded dingy and go from there. With our plan in motion and me bouncing around in the pitch-black trunk, Dave drove to school to do his usual pickup of classmates. Rita finally conceded to Dave's suggestion that she sit in the back seat for a change, and when everyone else had piled in, Dave roared out of the school parking lot. I quickly found myself chocking to death on the exhaust fumes seeping into the trunk. Through an empty speaker hole, I could see part of Rita's scarf covered head, but she sat there silently while I began to dread the stupidity of such a genius plan. When Dave's girlfriend Mary, from the front seat, asked if anyone wanted her apple, I shot my hand up through an empty speaker hole below the rear window and hollered, "I'll have it!" Rita jumped, bumping her head on the headliner, and shrieked, "Dave, someone's in your trunk!" After quite a commotion in the car, Dave obeyed Rita's demand to pull over. He wheeled his hot-rod, black Ford into the parking lot of the Shrine of the Immaculate Conception on the campus of Catholic University. The sound of car doors slamming told me the car was emptying. Finally, at Rita's persistence, Dave unlocked the trunk. I was momentarily blinded by the sudden burst of sunlight but glad to take a deep breath of fresh air. Swinging myself out of the trunk and getting vertical, I squinted Rita's way, bowed, and in my coolest tone announced, "Hi, I'm Mo Po, short for Most Popular!" (Someone at college started calling me that when they learned my given name was Maurice Patrick.). Rita's first look at me was not exactly what you'd call endearing. It was more like a mortified stare. Glancing at her friend Mary, she blurted, "God, what a weirdo!" They both giggled. Not exactly love at first sight, but hey, it was a start. Her stunned gaze melted into what seemed like an endless stare and slowly into the beginning of a faint smile. This freckled face girl with light brown hair poking from the edges of her scarf finally seemed to take a deep breath and introduce herself. For once, my pal Dave was right on. This Miss Rita could be a keeper. I couldn't help reading her mind: what kind of a clown would hide in a car's trunk to meet somebody? She had just entered the zany world of a joker whose previous antics included high school shenanigans like dropping a twenty foot banner reading, "Beat St. John's" from the top of the Washington Monument, and growing a two-story, multi-colored ice sickle from his second floor, college dorm window. After a bit of small talk, everyone climbed back into the car, and Dave proceeded to drive everyone home. Rita sat next to me in the back seat, and we exchanged awkward introductions. By the time we arrived at her home, we had agreed to go out on a double date with Dave and Mary. By the end of the weekend, we had also spent several hours holding hands and shivering outside the U.S. Capitol where we stood in a long line of mourners on East Capitol St. waiting our turn to pass by the bier of President Kennedy's body lying in state inside the Capitol rotunda. When I returned to school, we kept the mailman busy. In the fall of my senior year, we became engaged.

When Rita proudly showed off her new engagement ring to my Wheeling roommate Pete, he promptly quipped, "No wonder Casem's been saving all those Wheaties box tops!" Five months after my graduation, on the crisp fall morning of October 16, 1965, Rita and I were married in our St. Anthony Parish Church. Fr. Harold Hermley, OSF, a family friend from Philadelphia, presided at our wedding. His parting words to us on the altar were, "Go forth and have lots of little brats!" No problem. We'd both already agreed five kids would be fine.

That was the plan anyway.

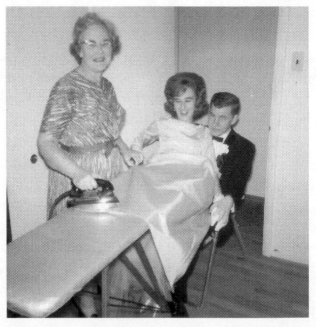

The freckle-faced girl named Rita and me, the guy she
found hiding in the trunk of a car, are off to her Senior
Prom, but not before her mom (Nanny) gets some last
minute wrinkles out of Rita's dress.

Chapter 3

All in the Family

The old saying when you marry someone you marry his/her family too is something I quickly learned. From the start, my in-laws, John and Marie Harner (Nanny and Pop), treated me like a son. The warmth and good humor between Rita's parents was something I was not used to. They had a significant influence on our young married lives. Nanny was the navigator while Pop, with his easygoing demeanor, did the driving. He worked his trade as a bookbinder at the Government Printing Office (GPO) on Capitol Hill. His thick hands worked effortlessly fixing or installing just about anything. Countless times, he had come to my rescue with his squinting smile and mild suggestion for me to "move over and let me have a look." Observing her mother's direct approach and her dad's dexterous hands, it quickly became obvious to me where Rita's pragmatic nature and mechanical talents came from. Unafraid to tackle and complete any job, my bride was always the first one under our sink imploring me to "Hurry up and find the !*#@ wrench!" Our families had a blast vacationing together. We would pool our funds, which Nanny would doggedly guard in her turquoise clutch purse, dispensing needed monies only when everyone else was present. Our wanderings took us from Canada to Florida and even a trip to California. Like most family vacations, the journey was just as entertaining as the destination. When Pop would make a wrong turn, a spontaneous eruption of flailing arms and twisting bodies meant everyone else in the car was scrambling for the map at the same time. While behind the wheel, Pop would sheepishly peek into the rear view mirror and interject his own appropriate concern, "Are you sure we remembered to bring the beer?" My first trip with my future in-laws happened during our engagement when I was invited to join them for a week in Wildwood, NJ. That was the first of a handful of times I'd share a bed with my future father-in-law. I suppose it was never a pretty sight, two grown men tossing and tugging at a shared blanket while snorting like a couple of feuding rhinos. On this particular trip, our tiny Wildwood, upstairs flat shared a common bathroom with the neighboring unit. Accessing the bathroom required stepping outside onto a small porch. Pop and I were on the pullout couch in the living room when I was awakened by nature's dreaded call. Stumbling to my feet in my skivvies, in the dark, I made my way to the front door and carefully stepped outside and entered the bathroom. Upon returning, I was startled to discover I had managed to lock myself out. My only thought was, "Well, so much for wonder boy's good standing with the in-laws! What's my soon-to-be mother-in-law going to say when she spies Mikie putting on a show outside in his underwear?" After a series of soft knocks on the front door, my heart sank as Nanny appeared in the doorway with her mouth aghast. Her startled voice quickly melted into a mother's concern. "What on earth? Mikie, get in here before you catch your death of cold!" The Harner's deep faith and practical wisdom gave me an increasing respect for them. Saying the rosary in the car on our long trips reminded me of my Mom's similar devotion. The seed had been planted for a practice, which in time, Rita and I eagerly embraced. Another custom in the Harner home was occasionally inviting clergy over for Sunday dinner. At one time or another, all the priests at St. Mark's parish made themselves comfortable around Nanny and Pop's dining room table. Each of these guys felt at home puffing a cigarette, sipping a beer or sharing silly things they did as kids. Nanny and Pop were teaching us an unwitting lesson: the humanity of us all. It could not get much better than great company and Nanny's scrumptious meals.

Like his Dad, Rita's older brother, Donnie, worked at GPO. Meeting Don and his wife Sue was like being with old friends I had known a long time. Like his sister, Donnie's engaging personality and mechanical traits came straight from his parents. With both of our families growing up in northeast DC, from the start, we always enjoyed each other's company. The biggest bond between Donnie and I grew over the twenty some years he and I spent together hunting white tail deer in southern MD. For a quarter of a century, Donnie patiently tried to transform me into a decent deer hunter. Traipsing around before dawn in the woods and expansive tobacco fields of a spectacular Charles County farm, Donnie tried teaching me how to carefully swing the barrel of my 870 Remington around, look down the barrel through the sites and then squeeze the trigger. He tried; I tried, but come day's end, the results were pretty predictable. At dusk, the setting sun would bid us all a fond adieu by casting its shimmering, yellowish-red veil across the Potomac River. Back in the barn, the fellow who was humming a Weylon Jennings tune and deftly wielding his Bowie knife to gut his latest six pointer was always Donnie, and the dude outside in the cowboy hat, the one leaning against Donnie's Ford Ranger, sharing another woeful tale with the guys about the big one that got away was me. Suffice it to say, everyone knew from the scores of big buck horns decorating the walls of Donnie's den who was the Davey Crockett and who was the tag along kid brother.

Waving my sheepskin proudly in the air at my Wheeling graduation, I am sure more than a few of the familiar, beaming faces around me were thinking, when is the kid going to get a job? At that moment, I realized that I was now paying the price for all those times I thought playing flag football in the mud with my buddies was a lot more fun than interviewing with the visiting employment recruiters up at Swint Hall. At last, a few weeks before our wedding, I spotted an opening for a furniture salesman at a store on upper Fourteenth St. in northwest Washington. I thought it might have been a calling for some, but it was not exactly what I had in mind after four years of college and all those summers working construction. Nevertheless, I swallowed my pride and went to work. A month or so into this new world of sofas and credenzas, the owner called me into his office to inform me they had decided to let me go because of "poor productivity." (I had a hunch things weren't going swimmingly because the previous few days I was told to wear old clothes to work so I could help the maintenance man paint the front of the store.) While facing my new bride (and in-laws) with my disappointing saga, my initial short-lived attempt at being the breadwinner was actually a relief. I had grown weary of playing this game of charades with our store customers. Each morning before opening the store, we busily glued arms onto chairs and slid matchbook covers under wobbly table legs. Then we were expected to lie to the customers about our "fine merchandise." By now, Rita had gotten a position as a bank teller where my life-long pal and former next-door neighbor, Ralphie Neilson worked. I was back to scouring want ads in *The Post* for just a few days when the mailman dropped off his infamous invitation.

Uncle Sam Wants You!

It was my draft notice which had been delayed by my four-year college deferment. Rita and I were expecting it sooner rather than later. It would put life on hold for a while. We knew it meant Viet Nam, but we would do what we had to do. Many of my buddies were already there. We had recently attended the emotional funeral at Arlington National Cemetery of a Gonzaga and Wheeling alum and my close friend Tom Reardon, USMC 2nd Lt. A week or so after receiving my draft notice, at 4:30 am, I found myself packed in a busload of recruits and other draftees rumbling up the B-W parkway to the Armed Forces Examining and Entrance Station at Fort Holabird located in a South Baltimore industrial area near Dundalk. We were told to bring all medical records, so I obliged with a small satchel that included doctor reports of my poor vision (unsuitable for driving) and medical records detailing my history of intermittent kidney issues dating back to birth. Around midnight, I was back in DC with my official US Army Classification: 1Y, meaning medically not fit to serve but not quite 4F, meaning completely unfit to serve. Or as a portly sergeant put it, "Don't you worry none boy. We need more cannon fodder, we'll find you!"

Chapter 4

Capitol Hill: Old Places, New Faces

In early November 1965, Mom's phone rang. It was Joe Bruno, an old family friend. Joe happened to inquire how I was doing, and she filled him in. Mom called to say Joe would be contacting me. Joe was a staff member at the White House when Dad first met him a few years earlier at the U.S. Capitol. In 1962, the year before he died, Pop had been detailed as a Metropolitan Police Detective to assist the U.S. Capitol Police and Secret Service guarding President Kennedy. It was part of a security beef up at the U.S. Capitol building following a recent unheard of gunshot episode in the Senate gallery. (Our family has a large picture of Pop standing next to President Kennedy in the U.S. Capitol rotunda). Joe called me and suggested I contact a Mrs. Portner, who was the Secretary to the Librarian of Congress. Joe knew Mrs. Portner from when he worked at the Library. I phoned Mrs. Portner, and an interview was set up. She offered me an entry-level GS-3 clerk position, which I eagerly accepted, a rather unremarkable introduction to a very remarkable place, The Library of Congress.

The Library was established by an act of Congress in 1800 when President John Adams signed a bill providing for the transfer of the seat of government from Philadelphia to the new capital city of Washington. The legislation described a reference library for Congress only, containing "such books as may be necessary for the use of Congress—and for putting up a suitable apartment for containing them therein . . ." The original Library was housed in the new Capitol until 1814 when the invading British burned the Capitol, destroying the contents of the small library. Congress accepted retired President Thomas Jefferson's offer to replace the library with his own personal collection of over 6,000 books. Jefferson envisioned the library to someday become a universal resource center. With the establishment of the Copyright law in 1870, the Library's collection grew to include maps, prints, photographs and sheet music; therefore, more space was then needed. In the late nineteenth century, Congress approved construction for a separate Library building in Italian Renaissance style to be named after Jefferson. The new Library opened its doors to the public on November 1, 1897, amidst much fanfare as a glorious national monument, hailed as the world's largest, costliest and safest library.

My first day on the job, co-workers Bobby Dove and Jimmy (JB) Broderick welcomed me to my own underwhelming duties at the Library which included filing the Librarian's correspondence and sorting and delivering the mail to the other departments around the Library (LC). I quickly discovered the labyrinth of tunnels connecting LC's buildings and an even larger maze that tied the Senate and House office buildings to the Capitol. I also had loads of time to gaze out one of our office's enormous arched windows. For the umpteenth time, I'd study the Greek architecture of the Supreme Court Building across the street or watch a gaggle of tourists head down East Capitol St. toward the Capitol. On one such watch, it occurred to me that having grown up in DC just how much time I had actually spent around Capitol Hill without ever giving it much thought. How often had I been inside and out of the Capitol? There was the Mall; how many Saturdays did Mom drag us three kids down there for CYO football games, or when relatives visited, we'd all climb aboard a green and tan Capitol Transit streetcar to ride down to the Mall for the Fourth of July fireworks. Just up North Capitol St. sat my alma mater Gonzaga High School, and across from the Capitol was the newly completed Sam Rayburn House Office Building where I spent those blistering hot summers as a laborer. Right out that LC window on East Capitol St. was where Rita and I walked by that November evening two years earlier, holding hands for the first time, and freezing our buns off along with all those other folks in line to view Kennedy's flag draped casket in the rotunda.

Pushing my squeaky-wheeled mail cart up and down the Library's ornate marble-floored hallways with arched, gold leaf painted ceilings, the thought rarely left me: four years of college, a couple thousand dollars in debt, English Literature degree, what was wrong with this picture? This was the world's largest library. There had to be a few challenging jobs. Maybe someone around here was trying to hang the moon, and they were looking for a guy to hold the ladder. My reverie of those earlier comings and goings around Capitol Hill and my current unexciting chores at the Library bore no hint of what was about to unfold. I would soon embark on a thirty-some year journey with a team of pioneers who would transform forever the way Thomas Jefferson's Library conducted its business.

I was trying to dislodge another paper jam at the Xerox machine one day while this chatty fellow with a dress shirt pocket full of pens and pencils waited patiently. Introducing himself as Jay Cunningham, we struck up a conversation, and he informed me that he worked in LC's Information System Office (ISO) across the street in the Adams Building. The mission of their office was to conduct a feasibility study to automate the entire Library of Congress. He suggested that with my college major, I might be interested in one of their entry-level automation positions. They were looking for a good tech writer. A few months later, I accepted a promotion to a GS-4 computer technician. I found my new job title a bit misleading since I knew nothing about computers. That would change soon enough. Thanks to bosses like Sam Snyder and Henrietta Avram, I was invited into the exciting new world of "data processing." The unselfish spirit of colleagues like Ken Pittman, Arlene Whitmer and Pat Parker, who took me under their collective wing, helped me get settled into tech writing. My assignments began with doing the dirty work most programmers retreated from, documenting their software. It quickly expanded to computer operation guides, end-user manuals and system design documents. Being surrounded by so many talented folks who allowed me to learn alongside them was truly humbling. I soon found myself immersed in the technical world, joining my colleagues taking graduate courses in the evening at the Department of Agriculture where we learned emerging programming languages and the latest operating systems. After work, I would walk the mile or so down the street to class while that evening Rita would bundle up and faithfully drive from our suburban MD apartment downtown to pick me up after class. We would arrive home late and go straight to bed: a routine that continued intermittently for several years. Work hard, play hard became the mantra of me and my colleagues. What started as an occasional beer after work gradually evolved into a post-work ritual at the *Tune Inn*, a Capitol Hill landmark and our pub of choice. Meanwhile, Rita was growing weary of holding dinner, and her increasing annoyance with me triggered unpleasant flashbacks of my father's same antics and the turmoil it caused in our home: a situation I never wanted my family to experience.

As a Precinct Detective with the Washington DC
Metropolitan Police Dept., Dad was assigned to be part of a
beefed up security detail at the U.S. Capitol. He is pictured
here (far right with white hanky in pocket) inside the Capitol
rotunda as President Kennedy (left center) passes by.

Chapter 5

Why Have You Abandoned Us?

Six months after we married, Rita became pregnant. We were beside ourselves with joy. Rita was about five months along when I talked her into joining me and my pal JB from work for a night at Rosecroft Race Track. She knew nothing about the trotters, but I insisted this was a good time to learn. Our fun evening out at the track turned out to be memorable, but for the wrong reasons. By the third race, the three of us were jammed together along the rail as the horses thundered down the homestretch. As the crowd screamed wildly, I turned to my wife, but she was gone. Glancing down, I gasped to find Rita sprawled out cold at my feet on the pavement. I looked at JB, and at a loss for words, I hollered, "I didn't think she'd get this excited!" A half-an-hour later in the Prince Georges County Hospital E.R., Rita had slowly come around. We were told she had hyperventilated and that her blood pressure had dropped. Mother and child both appeared to be fine, and with a giant sigh of relief, we were soon on our way home. Two months later, Rita began spotting. However, her obstetrician insisted there was no need for her to come in. "Just stay off your feet for a few days." A week later, I returned one evening after being out with some of my buddies. When I opened the front door of Rita's parents' home where she was spending the evening, I was shocked to be greeted by a sobbing wife and distraught in-laws. How terribly wrong the doctor was. That October evening in 1966, with the help of her Mom and two neighbor ladies, Betty Landi and Carol Jackson, Rita had suffered a miscarriage and delivered our stillborn baby boy. Our world had suddenly and cruelly crumbled. How could God do this? He knew how much we had wanted children!

Over the next few months, we managed to pick up the fragmented pieces of our lives, and I made a point of going home right after work. By then, Rita's delicious meals were a perfect excuse for why my trousers seemed to be getting a little snug. We gradually returned to socializing with friends like Ralphie and his wife Muff, Eddie "Spaghetti" Mattingly, and Dave and Carol Holden. We rotated weekends at each other's apartments, enjoying board games and a few libations. In October 1967, we found out that Rita was three months along in another pregnancy. Excited and frightened, we decided to hold off before sharing our good news. A short time earlier, Rita had gotten into painting ceramics with our friend Carol, and as a surprise Christmas present to her Mom, Rita had decided to make a complete set of mother-of-pearl porcelain Nativity figures. On the bottom of each figure, she inscribed one of the words from the phrase "Merry Christmas and Happy 1968 New Year from Rita and Mikie and ?" When her Mom had unwrapped each of the boxes and laid them out spelling our little surprise, the room exploded with shouts of joy. Soon everyone knew, and in February, I presented my colleagues at work with a chance to win some big bucks on when Rita would give birth to our first child. I called it Our New Baby Lottery. I concocted a grid where players could pick the date and sex of our baby. At two bucks a crack, winner took home the whole pot of $116. Tickets went like syrup at a pancake festival. Then it came: April

5, 1968, a day that will live forever! Martin Luther King, Jr. had been assassinated the previous day. Washington was torched by race riots, placed under Marshall Law and, of course, it was the day Rita decided to give birth. Our problem was we had to get to Providence Hospital in northeast Washington, which meant crossing into DC from our nearby Mt. Rainier, MD apartment. We were stopped at the DC line by National Guardsmen who made us all get out of Pop's blue Plymouth and open the trunk of his car. This blockade did not sit well with the Harner clan. Nanny began ranting at the young soldiers that they should all be ashamed of themselves for stopping a young woman about to give birth. Meanwhile, Rita leaned against me moaning and holding her belly. The usually docile Pop growled, "This is a bunch of malarkey because we ain't at war here, so get out of my way so I can get my daughter to the hospital!" The confounded troops stared at one another and after a momentary conference put their rifles at rest and waved us on. Back in the car, Pop winked at me and confessed he was glad they had not confiscated the case of beer he had just bought that was in the trunk. Roaring into the hospital parking lot, we hurried Rita into the E.R. About two hours later, Dr. Richard Kirchner (a Gonzaga alum himself, now looking forward to retirement) who had also delivered Rita, pushed open the waiting room door and peeked in where about six of us were waiting anxiously. He proudly announced, "Looks like you're ready for a hand of gin out here . . . she's a girl! A little scrawny, but she'll be fine." And so our beautiful, red haired daughter Tammy Lynn had sprung into our lives. Since she was only four and a half pounds, Tammy was placed in an incubator for two days. When she tipped in at five pounds, we exuberantly toted our new daughter home. Meanwhile, my pal Ken Pittman, a richer man by $116, shared our joy.

Like all new parents, life quickly became busier with diapers, baby bottles and car seats. Our family of three needed more space, so we moved around the corner into a first floor two-bedroom apartment.

My Mom's health had been declining, and a small, portable oxygen tank and her rosary accompanied her everywhere. On July 1, 1968, the MD State Legislature outlawed one of Mom's favorite past times, the slot machines. That same day, at the age of fifty-eight, she passed away. By then, my brother Tommy had followed in dad's footsteps and joined the Metropolitan Police Department as a Patrolman. (Three years earlier, he'd married his attractive wife Shirley and won a $5 wager with me that he'd beat me to the altar.) When Tommy was on day shift, we would run into each other after work for a few cold ones at the Kaywood Deli just down the street from our apartment. Once again, Rita began running short of patience holding dinner for me. Soon, Rita and I found ourselves pre-occupied with looking for our first dream house. In August of 1970, our dream came true. It was a modest 1940's blue and white shingled colonial in the nearby tree-lined community of Green Meadows. By now, with two children of their own, Tommy and Shirley were also looking for a house. As luck had it, not long after moving into our home, the house next door came up for sale, and my brother and his family became our new neighbors. The excitement of having our own house magnified when we found out that Rita was pregnant again. Tammy was almost three when we informed her that she would soon have a new baby brother or sister. Not wanting to know the baby's sex, we painted the small, upstairs spare bedroom a mint green. Sadly, one morning Rita found herself spotting, and two days later, she miscarried. We lost our second child. Numbed with grief, we would find ourselves silently sitting on the couch for long periods of time, sobbing into each other's arms. Broken-hearted and angry, we did not realize that we had yet to hit rock bottom.

After moving into our house, we transferred to Saint Mark parish in Hyattsville where our spiritual life rarely extended beyond the usual rituals: grace before meals and Sunday Mass. Our Pastor had learned of our recent miscarriage, and after Mass he offered a sincere "chin up" condolence. However, his well-intended sympathy came across as aloof. Then again, how could he feel our agony? How could any priest? One Sunday, we spotted an article in the bulletin welcoming volunteers to help with the upcoming Christmas bazaar. It piqued our interest, and we attended a session where we met several parents about our age. The Franks, the Lewis family, and several others introduced themselves and assured us that spinning a wheel of chance or selling fifty fifties wasn't brain surgery. The important part was to have some fun while helping to raise funds for the parish. Voila! We were off and running. For the next six years, come November, we were the caretakers of the popular "Dip 'N Win" booth at St. Mark's Christmas bazaar. Sharing the same spiritual values, bumps in the road, and similar stupid antics, our new group of friends slowly began lifting us from our emotional and spiritual doldrums. Before long, we had all become extended family to one another.

In the spring of 1971, some of my new buddies up at church began talking about joining the Knights of Columbus and asked if I was interested. I knew my dad had been a Knight, but other than the fact that they worked bingo, I did not know a lot about the organization. I had seen K of C banners all around the parish extolling the Order's principles of charity, unity, fraternity and patriotism. My chums and I were invited to attend a membership recruitment meeting where we learned that as the world's largest Catholic Men's fraternal organization, the Knights of Columbus offered volunteer manpower and financial assistance in support of the church and those in need everywhere, regardless of gender, race or creed. We filled out our applications, and on March 4, 1971, my friends and I took our First Degree and joined the other 1,200 members of Council 2809 in College Park, MD. Over the following several months, we advanced to our Second and Third Degree Exemplifications. The council's largest fundraiser, bingo, found a new team of volunteers when Brother Knights like Ben Lewis, Roman Dingler, Jim Carey and I became weekly fixtures at the hall working the council's Thursday evening session. We also began volunteering for Operation LAMB (Least Among My Brothers), a K of C State run program where all monies raised go directly to benefit physically and mentally handicapped children. Wearing our recognizable yellow aprons and giving away Tootsie Rolls, the Knights stand in public places and are familiar figures at storefronts soliciting donations on behalf of children with special needs. Alongside my Brother Knights, for the first time in my life, I also began volunteering at the local soup kitchen and visiting indigent neighborhoods where we distributed blankets, coats and Thanksgiving baskets. Entering these unchartered waters was an eye opener, realizing how very fortunate I had been and what I had been taking for granted. Nevertheless, I was totally unprepared for the priceless, joyful spirit and unwavering faith so many of these unheralded souls offered us in return.

With a renewed hope that we could do this, Rita and I decided we would not give up our dream of having more children. In the summer of 1974, Rita became pregnant a fourth time. But once again, God had His own plan. At a little over four months, Rita miscarried, and we lost our third child, and a year later, another miscarriage meant the loss of a fourth child. "Unbelievable!" we cried out loud in our loneliness, asking God, "Why have you abandoned us?" Phrases like "It was God's will . . . it happened for the best" even from our close friends now only resonated like the repeated, hollow bonging of a ghostly bell in a distant tower somewhere, tolling for yet another child we would never hold. Our response to God and nature was out of pain and rebellion, "Okay God, if you don't want us to have any more children, we'll do our part. We'll make sure we won't have any more." Thus, we shifted gears: goodbye "rhythm", hello birth control. Tammy was almost ten years old in early spring of 1978 when we discovered Rita was, uh oh, pregnant a sixth time. We honestly did not know whether to laugh or cry. Incredulously, our brief joy was short lived when we endured yet another ungodly miscarriage, and lost our fifth child. Nothing could dam the tears that streamed down our cheeks. Trying to grapple with what the Church endorsed about procreating life left us emptied and angry with our faith. Rita and I both underwent physical exams to determine if some underlying physical condition was the cause of our miscarriages. None was found. However, the urologist who thoroughly examined me confirmed something Rita and I were both aware of but a reality I had chosen to push to the back in my memory closet, perhaps hoping it would just go away. One of my kidneys was working a lot harder than the other kidney, which was shrinking. The doctor went on to inform me that my ongoing, intermittent urinary tract infections were due in large part from this congenital condition. While my current kidney function was in the normal range, the doctor said he would not be surprised if, at some point down the road, I would be facing complete kidney failure.

For a number of years, an old college chum Bill Mundie had been doing our taxes. One evening at his home, his wife, Cathy, mentioned a program they had gotten involved with called Marriage Encounter (M.E.). Even the name scared me. Cathy pointed out that the goal of M.E. was to improve communication in marriage. I piped up that that was certainly not our problem. Rita suggested it would be worth a try, so we did. Moderated by two married couples and a priest, the format of the weekend divided sessions into presentations, reflections and individual time alone. One of the weekend exercises asked us to write a love letter to our spouse. Many years earlier, when I was at school, we had eagerly done just that. Now, as I sat in a corner, pen in hand, I took a deep breath and thought, no problem, "I'll make it funny." However, all of a sudden I found myself pondering, what was going on with the lump in my throat and the watering eyes? "Get a grip, Casem. Oh crap," I thought, "I'm going to start bawling." Sure enough, after all these years, the nit-wit who hid in the trunk of the car was once again, ever so slowly, pouring out his heart to the freckled face brunette who just stood there in disbelief and stared at him. Just as in past letters he wrote to her almost daily, when he was away at school, that same guy was now writing another letter to her, reliving those same words—about their dreams, how they would persevere through everything together and telling her once again how very much he loved her. As the weekend activities drew to a close, and everyone was busy lugging their suitcases outside, the hotel elevator abruptly decided to take a sabbatical of its own. This untimely respite by Mr. Otis's marvelous invention caused quite a commotion, particularly among those three or four other couples who were stuck with us inside the car between floors until the local fire department came to our rescue. Our nerve-wracking and relatively unromantic three-hour interlude in the dark, however, did little to dampen our otherwise enriching weekend experience.

M.E. was a turning point for us. The program laid out "rules" for fighting fair in marriage: when you disagree, stay on the point of disagreement; don't bring up old stuff; there's nothing unmanly (or unwomanly) about saying "I love you" to your spouse every single day; and spend meaningful time together alone with each other and also with the family. It was practical advice that rang a bell with us but had gotten shoved into the background of our relationship between the baggage of self-pity and heartache. We went home feeling much better about ourselves and our attitude towards one another. It was a start but just a start. There were so many things to sort through and figure out. Five lost children and, like many laity in the church, our confusion over our matters of faith, like the lingering impact Vatican II Council still had from a decade earlier that seemed to turn upside much of what we'd been taught growing up as Catholics. We were exhausted, floundering in a sea of right versus wrong rip currents.

Enter Fr. Tom Wells.

Chapter 6

Accepting Human Brokenness

The voice resonating from the pulpit of Saint Mark's Church that summer Sunday in 1978 was that of our newly assigned, young priest named Fr. Tom Wells. His homily was brief, to the point and seemed to be aimed directly at Rita and me. "Sooner or later", he began, "most of us find ourselves facing some kind of horrific situation: a hopeless crisis which we neither anticipated nor are we able to handle alone. And in our human frailty, we cry out 'Why me?' Just as Jesus Himself did during His agony in the garden the night before His crucifixion, when He implored His heavenly Father, 'If it's Your Will, let this cup pass before me . . . but not as my will, but as your will be done!'" Continuing in a lowered voice, Fr. said, "So you see, we are never alone in our anguish. In His human form, through His Son Jesus Christ, God knows exactly what we're going through and how we feel. If we truly believe that, then we know He is always nearby, ready to lift us up. All we need to do is have the faith to invite Him in." Fr. Wells's closing remarks revealed a hint of his wit and engaging social nature. Clearing his throat, he leaned into the microphone and announced, "Oh, by the way, boys and girls, did Fr. tell everyone he simply loves good, home cooking?"

As had happened with countless other parish families, it only took a single invitation to Sunday dinner for this charismatic and compassionate priest to become a regular, welcomed visitor to our home. We quickly learned how much we had in common. Fr. Wells was two years younger than I, and we both grew up in the DC area. Right off, we enjoyed ribbing each other about graduating from archrival Catholic high schools. He was a "Johnnie Mop" from the Christian Brothers' St. John's Military High School while I was a Gonzaga Purple Eagle, hand molded by the good Jesuit Fathers. It didn't take long before Rita and I began pouring out our hearts to Fr. Wells about our anger with God, our ongoing despair and excruciating heartache with the loss of five children over the past several years. We told him we were certainly blessed to have our daughter Tammy who was now ten, but we had no answer to why God continued to punish us for simply trying to have more children. Weren't we following the Church's teaching about the purpose of marriage? For too long, we had grown weary of going through the motions of our faith, and we simply were worn out.

This remarkable priest took the time to patiently absorb our plight and ever so gradually offer us hope to find our way out of our spiritual graveyard. Fr. Wells gently reminded us how the core teachings of our Catholic Faith were based on the examples and teachings of Jesus Christ, the Son of God made man. Through His Son Jesus, God experienced human suffering, agony and rejection. By His own words, Jesus came to heal the sick, the broken, and through repeated examples in the life of His Son, God made it clear that it is only through our brokenness that we can be lifted up and made whole again. He noted examples like Jesus' blessing and breaking of the five loaves and fishes that fed thousands of people and His blessing and breaking of the bread at the Last Supper that becomes His body in the Sacrament of the Holy Eucharist that continues to nourish and sustain us some two thousand years later. Ultimately, Jesus Himself was broken at His Crucifixion on Calvary, and three days later, He rose from the tomb. These final acts of being broken, raised up and made whole again by the Son of God opened the gates of heaven and saved all of mankind from the brokenness of sin. Fr. Wells concluded by saying the bottom line for all of us is that before we can be truly open to being raised up, or to helping raise someone else up, we must first accept all human brokenness, both our own and others'. Fr. Wells's straightforward nature never allowed him to get bogged down in theological rhetoric. One of the deepest forms of human suffering, Fr. Wells told us, is the pain of loneliness that comes with the loss of a loved one who has died. This situation leaves us with an emptiness that seemingly cannot be filled and thus can shake one's faith tremendously. In the case of repeated losses over a period of time, quite understandably, the very foundation of our faith can be rocked. Again, in his uniquely compassionate but joyful manner, Fr. Wells reminded us that our Catholic Christian faith was not only rooted in believing that Jesus Christ died on the Cross for us, but also it was believing that in His Resurrection from the tomb, he *overcomes death for all of us* and opens the gates of Heaven forever for all true repentant believers. What we needed to do at this point in our own lives, he said, was cling with all our might to that tiny thread of faith still inside us from baptism, and just as with His own Son Jesus, God would not abandon us.

He effortlessly fit all the pieces together, meshing the paradoxes and disconnects of life with the life of Christ and the Mysteries of our Catholic faith. This appearance of this remarkable priest in our lives re-ignited a candle of hope which for too long had been extinguished under our accumulated rubble of broken dreams and self-pity. As we slowly began picking up the pieces and inching ourselves forward, Fr. Wells wasted no time challenging us to grow in our faith. His first suggestion, to get involved in the annual Right-To-Life March, immediately energized us. Come January, from that year on, we eagerly accompanied our fellow parishioners and Brother Knights, joining the hundreds of thousands of others on the Mall downtown. There, our collective voices sang out loud and clear on behalf of the silenced voices of the millions of innocent, unborn children murdered by abortion.

Within a few months of his arrival at St. Mark's, Fr. Wells announced that he would like to form a spiritual reflections group for married couples. Evidence that our parish was starving for such a venue came in the form of the fifty or so couples who showed up at the first scheduled meeting. It was quite a sight at the home of the couple who offered to host our first meeting. People jammed in every corner of every room on the first floor, people stacked up and down the staircase, and they crowded together on the front porch peering through the windows and the open front door. Perched on a stool in the middle of the living room sat Fr. Wells with his bright blue eyes beaming and was obviously in shock over the unexpected throng. His booming voice trumpeted us to attention. "Well, well, well, thank you all for coming out tonight. But frankly, this is a bit more folks than I had in mind." The walls ricocheted with laughter. He quickly laid out a few ground rules. No kiddies please. This would not be a problem solving session. Monthly meetings would last no longer than an hour. We would pick a book of reflection and share our thoughts on it, and of course, everyone would bring munchies and a few cold beverages to share at the end of the evening. He finished by saying that smaller was better, and if need be, multiple groups of five or six couples could be formed. By about the fourth session, the throng had shrunk to six couples, including folks we had met earlier through the church bazaar. New faces like the Azarenkos, Ken and Terri Stark, and later the Berards rounded out the official St. Mark's Couples Group. One of our early topics of discussion was civil religion, addressed by Fr. David Knight in his book, *His Way*. As Knight explains, civil religion is the acceptance by society of immoral actions simply because everybody (or nearly everybody) does them. The lines between right and wrong quickly become blurred when seemingly small actions that "don't hurt anyone else" like cheating on taxes, spending hours at work playing on the computer or glancing through porn become acceptable. Inevitably, major atrocities such as legalized abortion (since it can be performed in a sterile environment as opposed to a back alley trashcan somewhere) become perfectly acceptable by a so-called civilized society. Fr. Wells reminded Catholic Christians dealing with civil religion was certainly nothing unique to today's society. When Christ began His public ministry and gathered His apostles and first disciples around Him, from day one, whenever they denounced things like adultery, stealing or self-indulgence, they faced ridicule and rejection by civil and religious leaders alike. Fr. Wells concluded by pointing out that if we truly call ourselves Catholic Christians, we must be willing to be "fools for Christ." Occasionally, our dialogue over a topic would cause our reverend moderator to abruptly toss his head back in mock frustration and proclaim, "Oh! Ye of little Faith!" Fr. Wells was always tossing spiritual nuggets our way. On personal suffering for example, he commented that someone's suffering and even his/her death can actually draw others closer to God. Whenever we pray for anyone, we draw ourselves closer to God. Also, God is especially pleased when someone who might not otherwise be inclined to have any conversation at all with God decides to say a prayer for another person.

Our Couples Group get-together activities quickly expanded to include anniversary and birthday celebrations and even vacationing. Our family and the Franks, for instance, enjoyed the challenges of the great outdoor sport of tent camping. We could break our plastic tent stakes with the best of them. Bang! Bang! Pop! Bang! Bang! Snap! Buried tree root, bedrock, didn't matter, we'd find it, and another tent stake would go flying in half a dozen pieces. One of our favorite campgrounds was Germantown State Park located in the Appalachian Mountain range of western MD (where the coldest temperature in the state is recorded). It was on one such visit that little Timmy Frank had his first close encounter in the middle of the night with a wild black bear. Inside the tent with his parents Betsy and Larry, the startled young boy woke his father to nervously inquire, "Is that a bear outside?" "No son," yawned his dad, "Go back to sleep. That's just Mr. Casem snoring."

Fr. Wells also took the Couples Group to Ireland, a place he had visited often and the homeland of my paternal grandmother Mary Cunningham Casem. Our first stop on the Emerald Isle was Bunratty Castle and a few mandatory goblets of warm mead. Wow! Over the next week, we did not miss much, including windswept vistas of the coast and a bent over backwards kiss of the Blarney Stone. One stop found us at a thatched roof pub in the hamlet of Sligo, not far from the border of Northern Ireland. Our bus parked at the front door, and in a flash, we were all lined up at the bar, slurping down our pints of Guinness. I happened to ask the barmaid if there were any Cunninghams nearby. In her thick brogue, she replied, "Sure, there in be a family right there across the lane." Excited at her response, I blurted, "Wow, my Grandma was a Cunningham, and she was born in County Down. How far is that from here?" Without warning, the barmaid's smile curled into a ferocious frown, and she began flailing the bar rag above her head. Startled by the sudden commotion, the sleeping black dog on the dirt floor raised his head and sprung to his feet barking. The elderly woman continued her rage, "Get out o' me pub ye scoundrels, and 'n ne'er set foot in here ah-gen!" Outside, Fr. Wells sarcastically thanked me for getting us all kicked out, and quipped that in all his visits to Ireland, he had never been booted out of a pub. As we re-boarded our bus, Fr. Wells cautioned me with a wink, "Casem, do us all a favor. When we get to (the Shrine at) Nock, please don't play with the rosaries."

None of us ever imagined that when we all decided to become part of a St. Mark's parish spiritual reflection couples group that our friendships would last a lifetime.

In the spring of 1979, some of my Saint Mark buddies invited me to go on a weekend retreat sponsored by the men's Holy Name Society (I wasn't a member). I was quite familiar with the location on the banks of the Potomac River in southern MD. It was adjacent to the sprawling farm where my brother-in-law Donnie and I annually stalked white tail deer. Nearby was *Pope's Creek Crab House*, a familiar haunt for all of us since our teens. Two decades earlier, our Gonzaga senior high school class spent a weekend retreat at this bucolic setting in rural Charles County sixty miles south of DC. This time, however, our weekend program was an abbreviated version of Ignatius Loyola's four week Spiritual Exercises. Ignatius believed that anyone seeking God need not wait for visions, but in an intelligent and humble way had only to invite God in. Then with God's grace, one could find God in all things and be heroes by bringing God to all people. Each retreat participant had his own small, clean room with a window, bed, sink and toilet. Except at meals, silence was observed throughout the retreat. The spiritual exercises involve mind, memory, will and imagination. The format consists of daily Mass, reciting the rosary as a group, a series of spiritual readings by the Retreat Master, quiet reflections, opportunities for Confession and some free time. I found myself taking this second trip to Loyola a lot more seriously now than my previous visit as a rambunctious, hotshot high school senior. Now, God and I had several heart-to-hearts. In my tiny room, I cried alone and begged for His guidance. Strolling alone on the winding paths through the retreat grounds heavily wooded landscape, I silently enjoyed His companionship in the gentle breeze and occasional wildlife that scurried nearby. Heading back home Sunday afternoon, I found myself pondering the weekend's events and the unexpected closeness to God that had enveloped me. Maybe God hadn't given up on us. The parade of recent events in our lives—joining the Knights, Marriage Encounter, Couples Group, and now this retreat—it was as if He was taking us by the hand and leading us somewhere. Maybe He had been knocking on the door all along, but we had just finally recognized it was time we open it and let Him in.

Chapter 7

Welcome to Our World

Motivated by what we had learned at M.E., Rita and I incorporated some of their suggestions into our home life. Each day after work, Rita and I made time for ourselves, usually by going outside and strolling around the block for half hour or so, exchanging how things had gone for each of us that day. We also picked Sunday to have a family night. Together with Tammy, who was now eleven, we spent that time sharing exciting things that may have happened, playing a board game and enjoying some cookies and soda. It was a start, and Rita and I agreed, at least we were trying. Slowly, our new routine brought a renewed sense of normalcy, and with it some much longed for happiness.

Soon after our M.E. experience and my retreat at Loyola, we were seated in our usual pew at St. Mark's 8 a.m. Sunday Mass that warm June day in 1979. However, I was daydreaming about our upcoming vacation week at Ocean City while I sat with Rita and Tammy. I was startled by someone squeezing my left hand. It was, of course, Rita seated next to me. She turned and whispered, "What do you think about taking her in?" Oblivious to the reason for her question, I mumbled, "Taking who in?" She rolled her eyes with that familiar look of disgust. "Didn't you hear what Fr. Wells said?" Fr. Wells was nicknamed "Boomer" for a reason. Paying attention to his homily was normally not an issue, but this particular Sunday, my mind had carried me along with it a hundred or so miles east where I found myself on the boardwalk, devouring a pile of hot steamed crabs and washing them down with an iced cold mug of beer. My imaginary trip had kept me from hearing Fr. Tom Wells's invitation to the congregation to consider helping an unwed, pregnant teen who was looking for a place to stay. Little did we realize, however, that our dear friend Fr. Wells was just getting started changing our lives forever. Waiting our turn in line, we shook hands and told him we would seriously consider taking the young teen into our home. Without hesitation, he looked me in the eye and, jabbing his finger into my chest, proclaimed, "I promise you will never regret doing this!"

Rita and I went home and began discussing it and praying over the possibility of actually doing it. Initially, Rita was more enthusiastic about the idea of bringing in a complete stranger than I was. We discussed it with Tammy, and she thought it would be great. I kept thinking about all the "what ifs" and feebly protested, "But I won't be able to run around upstairs in my skivvies!" Rita gave that familiar tilt of her head and shot back, "and that would be a good thing!" causing us both to crack up. Fr. Wells's earlier words echoed in my mind. "God showed us through His Son how much he wants to help us, and He is always nearby, ready to lift us up; all we need to do is invite Him in." We prayed as a family to guide us in our decision. Our eight-year-old beagle Barney (actually, Barney Rubble Beagle Bubble) sensed something was up. When he kept looking quizzically at us, we shared our exciting news with him. Before leaving for our week vacation in Ocean City, we phoned Fr. Wells to tell him we would help the young girl. He roared with delight and said the young girl's name was Theresa, and he would be getting back to us as soon as we returned from Ocean City. During our stay at the beach, the three of us got more excited each day about our upcoming venture. We again prayed together and told God that we would do our part and leave the rest in His hands.

It never fails. Just when pulling into the driveway, the phone starts ringing in the garage. That's what happened as we arrived home from our week at the beach. I managed to pick up the receiver before the caller hung up. A voice identified himself as Fr. Mike Wilson, a friend of Fr. Wells.

The following is Theresa's description of the next five months.

"Two Catholic priests, one pregnant teenager, and a married couple sit in a church pew one Sunday morning. Minus the 'walk into a bar' part, it sounds like the opening to a Catholic joke. In reality, it begins an intersection of lives that vividly illustrates the loving hand of God and the joy of realizing His purpose. Midway through the summer of 1979, I was midway through an unplanned pregnancy. As the oldest of five children, the pregnancy led to emotional upheaval in my home. Once I completed the school year (and high school), it became clear that it would be better for my younger siblings if I lived elsewhere as the pregnancy continued. With no real plan, I spoke to Fr. Mike Wilson at my local parish for alternatives. Fr. Mike had met with me early in my pregnancy, and, once again, he was quite comforting. After several days, he called me with an offer. Fr. Tom Wells, pastor at St. Mark's church in Hyattsville, knew a couple at his church who was willing to open their home to me. Even though Fr. Wells had recently been an associate pastor at our church in Bowie, I had no idea what to expect. Once I met Mike and Rita, it seemed right to move forward.

"Strangely, I was not nervous that Saturday I moved into Mike and Rita's house. What I felt was an immediate sense of peace. Quickly, I realized the reason for that peace was the love that permeated their home. From my first days there, they made me part of their family. I was included in every outing, met every one of their equally kind friends, and shared some of the most entertaining dinners of my life around their table with those two priests and a favorite nun. One of my fondest memories was our Sunday evening, family prayer circle. Mike, Rita and my new eleven-year-old sister Tammy opened their hearts and minds to me and allowed me to enter into theirs. Rita cared for me physically and emotionally in a way I had not previously experienced. Many nights, she and I stayed up late talking about my future. I do not think I had spoken so openly with anyone before her. She listened to every joyful or fearful thought that I had on any given day. Both she and Mike provided much humor which helped me feel hopeful throughout those months.

On a perfect fall day in late October, with Rita as my labor and delivery coach, I gave birth to my beautiful son, Jonathan. When I held him for the first time, I knew I would never be able to adequately thank the Casem family for welcoming us with such love and acceptance. In yet another expression of that love, Mike and Rita agreed to become Jonathan's God Parents."

Hugging Theresa and giving little Jonathan a goodbye kiss as they left our home to resume the rest of their lives together was like saying so long to our own children. I was surprised by the feeling of sadness that came over me. We both felt an unexpected void in our home as we shut the front door behind us. We had no clue our sense of emptiness would be short lived. Before too long, we'd be welcoming another complete stranger into our home, this time coming from halfway around the world to live with us on a permanent basis. I popped open a Bud and slumped into my favorite chair. However, I felt perplexed why Fr. Wells's response to us about taking Theresa in kept swirling in my head.

"I promise, you will never regret this."

Theresa, me and Jonathan the day Theresa
brought Jonathan home from the hospital.

Jonathan's baptism was held at the original
Sacred Heart Catholic Parish Church in
Bowie, MD, one of the earliest
Jesuit missionary sites in America. Pictured
(left to right) are me, Rita, Jeff Palumbo
(Jonathan's father) and
Theresa holding Jonathan.

Chapter 8

Let the Dead Bury Their Dead

Never one to stand on formality, Fr. Wells seldom waited for a special invite to Sunday dinner or to watch part of a Redskin game. He would simply pop open the front door and announce, "Yoo-hoo! . . . Is anybody home? It's me. What's for dinner? Mind if I join ya'?" End of discussion. He had a certain routine whenever he came over. He'd head for the dining room, fish out his wallet and keys, plunk them down on the hutch, slip off his loafers, nudge them together on the floor, and head for the kitchen. If something was cooking, he'd lift the lid off each pot, take a deep sniff and declare, "Mm-mm that smells delish. Got a Bud?" Before the meal, we would share a beer or two. Within half-an-hour after eating, he would abruptly jump to his feet (often in the middle of a conversation) and announce, "Gotta go. I promised (so and so) I'd drop by." With a single swipe, he'd gather his keys and wallet, slip back into his loafers and be out the door with a "See ya!" There was no telling how many Mikie and Ritas he'd promised to visit that day. We never asked; it was none of our business. The sudden appearance and abrupt exit was part of his style. He couldn't help it; he was on a mission. His whole life was a mission, never staying in one place too long, very much reminding me of someone else: Jesus.

Fr. Wells was never bashful about borrowing Jesus' words to fit the occasion. Like the haymaker, he landed about a month or so after Theresa joined our family.

Rita and I were headed out the front door on our way to pay a visit to my parents' gravesites. Looking up, we saw the man behind the familiar smiling face galloping toward us. "Where ya' headed?" Fr. Wells quipped. When we informed him of our destination, without taking a breath, he retorted, "Oh, let the dead bury their dead. I have something much more important for you!" A few minutes later, the three of us were gathered around the dining room table. Taking a sip of his Bud and setting the bottle on the table, Fr. Wells cleared his throat, crossed his arms and began, "Have you ever thought about teaching CCD?" Rita and I looked at each other stunned. "What are you crazy?" I stammered. "We know nothing about teaching anything, and I have my hands pretty full." Game on. Father leaned forward, began rubbing his Budweiser back and forth between his palms and started, "Um, excuse me Mo-eese (his exaggerated pronunciation of my first name), don't you have a minor in Theology from Wheeling, and are you ever going to use it? This assignment should be a piece o' cake for you!" He was on one of his rolls, "Oh and I'd hardly call working Bingo one night a week at the Knights a busy schedule . . . and pardon me if I'm wrong but haven't you and your lovely wife here been teaching your own child all these years about your faith and you're now doing the same for Theresa?" We were speechless. I couldn't resist a meek volley, "Actually it was an English major and a double minor: Theology and Psychology." Unimpressed, my friend silently rolled his eyes. When we feebly offered to think about his proposal, he nodded knowingly that once again it was point, set, match, Fr. Wells. The visit might have lasted fifteen minutes. Going out the door, he turned and gave us his familiar victory wink and smile, "Should you decide to do this, keep in mind one thing. You may find this hard to believe but maybe once in a great while you may come across a youngster who actually doesn't want to be in your CCD class because he'd rather be outside playing ball. Don't get discouraged; resist your temptation to scream and bolt out of class. Re-ee-member, all you can really expect to do is plant a seed; leave the rest up to God. The next morning we opened the front door and on the stoop was a pile of Archdiocese of Washington CCD textbooks and planning manuals. Stuck inside the cover of the book on top was a note flapping in the breeze. Rita bent over, retrieved the note and read it aloud, "Look through these and you'll do just fine—Fr. Wells."

And so began our long-running and very busy chapter working side by side as Catechists. That September, we initiated our diligent, weekly CCD teaching cycle. Our regiment started Monday evening, using the class syllabus to prepare for that week's class; Friday was a quick review; Saturday was class; Sunday was time spent correcting homework and a quick review of how things went (or didn't); and Monday the drill started again. The routine was hardly "a piece o' cake", but surprisingly, we found it bolstered our own faith and strengthened our commitment to doing things together. For the next seventeen years—eight at Saint Mark's School in Hyattsville and nine at Saint Joseph's School in Beltsville, MD—we served as CCD volunteer elementary school team teachers in the Catholic Archdiocese of Washington. Emptying ourselves in the business of planting a few seeds of our Catholic faith into the hearts of our young students, we had opportunities to teach every grade except sixth. As any teacher can attest, there were many occasions when we did not want to be there any more than our students did, but somehow we all managed to muddle through. One week, little Phillip was pushing us to the wall with his smart aleck answers. Only after class did we find out from a sobbing Phillip that he hadn't gotten any sleep or dinner the previous evening because mom and her boyfriend were drunk and up all night arguing. It didn't take many such incidents to remind us of the awesome responsibility that had been entrusted to us. We had to somehow push aside the drudgery and keep in mind the reality: in many cases, we may have been the only link many of these children had to learning about God and our Catholic faith. More than a few times I saw myself out there in our audience, gazing wistfully out the window, my mind a zillion miles away while my second grade teacher, Sister Hillary, pranced back in forth up in the front of class hoping against hope to gain my attention (yes, Dorothy, God does have a sense of humor). Art Linkletter could have written his entire book in just one of our classes. Spontaneous laughter was never far off. One day, I quizzed our third graders with the usual, "What's your favorite Bible story?" As usual, studious Ronnie in thick, horned rimmed glasses shot up his hand. Nodding for him to answer, Ronnie stood erect, hands at his sides and almost shouting, proclaimed, "Nolan's Ark. That's when God got really ticked off at all the dinosaurs for eating everything in sight. So He asked this old guy Nolan to build a boat. I'm not sure if it was inboard or outboard, but anyway, it was big enough for Nolan and all the animals except the dinosaurs. Then God told them all to get on board, and He turned on the spigot real hard and flooded everything, including the dinosaurs. Then God sent out all the water sucking trucks, and they went around sucking up all the water, and Nolan and all the other animals were saved."

So it went from the fall of 1979 until spring of 1996. During that time, it was our privilege to spend our time trying to share the tenets of our Catholic faith with five hundred or so children. In the end, our munchkins taught us much more than we did them. Their energy and rambunctiousness kept us energized and on our toes. Their innocence and vulnerability humbled us. On rare occasions, a student's eyes would light up as they'd squeal, "Oh, I get it!" Witnessing these rare, spiritual transformations was like glimpsing clumsy caterpillars suddenly morphing into brilliant, colorful butterflies, swooning skyward for the first time, and carrying the rest of us along with them. Undoubtedly, those special moments were the icing on that "piece o' cake" our friend had mentioned years earlier.

One day Rita came home from work and told me that her boss at the Pastoral Center, Fr. Enzler, had invited us to participate as a presenting couple for the Archdiocese Pre-Cana Program. Unsure of what we might have once again been getting ourselves into, we decided to give it a try. Sharing our real life marriage experience with an audience of engaged couples, I suppose, got off to an awkward, bumbling start, but we soon found ourselves looking forward to these monthly, Sunday afternoon sessions and realized that once again, God had presented us with another opportunity to grow in our faith.

Chapter 9

Push a Button Down!

Rita and I had privately broached the subject of adoption off and on since our M.E. experience, but neither of us seemed ready to get serious about it, so the subject inevitably got dropped. Shortly before Theresa left our home, we spotted an article about adoptions through Catholic Charities that piqued our interest. The timing was right. We had already welcomed a stranger, now a beloved part of the family, Theresa, into our home, but she and her newborn would be leaving. God's bigger plan seemed to be unfolding before us, so we decided to take a serious look into adoption. All of a sudden, we could hardly quell our excitement. We investigated Catholic Charities' options and discovered that most of the children available at that time were African American infants or older children with serious health issues. Tammy was eleven, and we had decided that we were past the diapers and bottles stage with another child. Our goal was a Caucasian boy or girl around three years old. The emotional scars of losing five children never entirely dissipate, so we were honestly not inclined to knowingly pursue a child with special needs. We looked into U.S. adoptions, in general, and were discouraged to find the majority of these children came from foster care, typically coming from more than one home. Were we being too picky? It was 1979 and what few private adoptions were available were extremely expensive and more than a little risky. We chose not to go that route. Stunningly, our search for a son or daughter was going nowhere—again.

Enter a little Jewish lady named Sheri Simas.

We met Sheri in November through some mutual friends. A short, salt-and-pepper haired energetic woman, Sheri and her husband had recently adopted boy and girl siblings, ages four and five from South Korea. Sheri had become active in assisting folks with overseas adoptions through an organization in Colorado named Friends of the Children of Viet Nam (F.C.V.N.). This was a carry-over adoption facility from the Viet Nam war which helped place Vietnamese orphans with adoptive U.S. parents. Since the fall of Hanoi, F.C.V.N. had re-directed its operations to help place orphans from other Asian countries with prospective U.S. families. We had several meetings with Sheri and her husband. They shared their experience as well as references and literature about F.C.V.N. Through Sheri, we were made aware that adopting older children, especially where there was a cultural difference, such as with Asian children, a predictable percentage of adoptions did not work out because they would be unable to adjust and would then be sent back to their homeland. For that reason, at that time, the placement of Asian children with U.S. families required a one-year trial period before the family could proceed with the final adoption process in their state. After observing Sheri's children, we were hooked. By now, we decided on a boy. We would name him Andrew (after the apostle), and his middle name would be Thomas—after Fr. Wells. So we made it known: a little Korean boy aged three or so. By January 1980, through F.C.V.N., we contacted the orphanage agency in Seoul. Communications began: tons of paperwork and a home study were the required, official credentials. Back and forth it went and back and forth again, on and on. We sent the pictures they requested: shots of our home and pictures of any existing children and pets, pictures of the car, our son's new bedroom, pictures of all of us down at my sister Patty's home with her husband Uncle Bill and their three girls; they named it, we sent it. Weeks, then months went by, "we're working on it" was all we were told. Then a letter . . . "no three year old boys but an older boy, five . . . will that be okay?" We immediately replied yes, only to wait again. Another correspondence: "no five year old boys, how about a seven year old?" Our frustrations were mounting. At one point, I recall turning to Rita and telling her, "You watch. At this rate we're going to wind up adopting a thirty-five year old man!" Finally, (and ironically) almost nine months to the day after the whole process with F.C.V.N had begun, we received "official" word and photographs of our nine-year-old son-to-be. He would be coming "very soon" flying from Seoul to Seattle to National (now Reagan National) Airport in DC. Our friend Sheri warned us that "very soon" could mean the day after tomorrow. The next day, Friday, we received a phone call that our son would be arriving with a contingent of other Korean adoptees and their escorts at 8 p.m. on Monday, November 10, 1980.

We had cleared our schedule as best we could, unsure of the exact date that our son would be arriving. We had sent him some matchbox cars and a black and orange Orioles baseball cap, but we had kept our cherished tickets to the Barry Manilow concert scheduled for that Monday evening at the Capitol Center as long as we could, just in case. When we called our friend Carol Halderman, she was delighted for us—and the tickets. Late Monday afternoon, on the day of our son's scheduled arrival, our mini caravan to National Airport gathered at our house. We told our pooch Barney to hang loose, and pretty soon, he would meet our newest family member, our son Andrew.

We ensured everybody had everything: cameras, Kleenex, Andrew's coat. Traveling in Pop's Plymouth wagon were Nanny and Pop, Rita, Tammy and me. In the VW bus behind us were our close friends, Tammy's "aunt" and "uncle" Ralph and Muff Neilson. Pretty much everybody was already bawling before we ever got into the vehicles. This time, they were tears of long-awaited joy. When the P.A. in the airport terminal announced the arrival of Andrew's flight, along with a swarm of other new parents in waiting, we hurried to nudge our way along the rope separating us from the stream of passengers exiting the airplane. One by one, the young children filed past us, clutching their escort's hand. While parents in waiting shouted and clicked away with their cameras, the faces of the Korean children who were old enough to walk spoke volumes: a mix of fright and anticipation. Each child wore an official name badge, identifying him/her and his/her escort. Finally, near the end of the long line, we spotted the young boy walking stiffly with the bright orange and black Oriole cap pulled firmly down barely above his eyes. We waved and hollered to his escort. Still holding his hand, she quickly walked over to us and smiled. We introduced ourselves, and after examining our identification, she stooped down to the young boy at her side whose eyes were fixed on the floor. After a few words in Korean, our son released his grip on his escort's hand and slowly lifted his head up towards us. One by one, we all bent down and hugged Andrew while the camera shutters continued to click around us. Rita and I had made a valiant attempt to learn some basic Korean words and phrases, but suddenly everything we had practiced seemed to have vanished. After a quick stop at the rest room, we headed outside into the frigid November air and our cars. When we arrived home, it was getting late, but we sat in the living room anyway: the whole caravan just kind of sitting there smiling at each other and trying to communicate with our new son. Once in a while, Andrew looked up and smiled. Among the items in the little satchel he carried was a small picture album we had sent him. Rita opened it and began showing him the picture and then pointing to the object. Barney had taken his position at the end of the couch which seemed to make Andrew pretty nervous. He would look at Barney and mutter something none of us understood and look down. We asked old Barn' to hop down, and Rita fixed a bowl of rice and biscuits that we all enjoyed at the dining room table. With that, everyone left, and at last, it was just the four of us and Barney. We took Andrew upstairs in the spare bedroom, which would be his. He looked around wide-eyed but said nothing. Rita had drawn our son's bath water, and the two of them headed for the tub. A short while later, they emerged from the bathroom; soon Rita and I were seated next to our new son on his bed. Andrew seemed to be captivated by his new pajamas, rubbing the legs and sniffing the sleeves. It was obviously something very new to him, just one of a zillion new things he would be encountering over the coming weeks and months. That first night was a sleepless venture for all of us. The idea of sleeping on a bed was completely foreign to Andrew. We would tuck him in and turn out the light, only to be awaken an hour or so later to his sobbing. Each time we returned to his room, he would be curled up on the rug on the floor. On our last visit, just before dawn, our nine-year-old son was seated on the floor crying uncontrollably; the light was turned on, and on the chalkboard we'd placed on the wall at one end of the room was the unmistakable drawing of the Korean flag. It hit us right between the eyes, a somber awakening for everyone. We had been cautioned about an adjustment period, but deep down, we thought it would not happen to us. What did we expect? Our son spoke no English, and we spoke little Korean. Faces of strangers making a fuss over him, sleeping in a bed, a dog in the house, running water inside the home . . . . a barrage of completely new and unsettling experiences for a nine year old and a cosmos apart from Pusan, South Korea where our son had been raised in a world of flooded rice paddies and buried jars of fermenting kimchee. This was just the beginning of a long and often painful journey for all of us to get through and to grow together as a family. Beginning early the next morning, the doorbell and phone never seemed to stop ringing. Relatives, friends, neighbors, everyone wanted to meet Andrew, and our son thought it was a good idea too because with most every visitor came a gift. Pretty soon, when the doorbell rang, Andrew would scamper to open it with one hand and extend his other palm upward anticipating the next present. Correcting him and apologizing to the incoming guest made little difference. Return callers did not bother him; he would hit them with the same routine again. Nevertheless, I will give Andrew credit, he would politely bow and in Korean thank the person(s) very much for the gift. Within a few weeks, there were toy trucks and motorcycles, soldiers, Frisbees and new clothes piled all around the family room. Eventually, the parade of well-intended folks bearing gifts came to a halt, allowing the arrival of some long-awaited tranquility.

Sister Agnes McCarthy, OHC had accompanied Fr. Wells in his assignment to our parish. She wore a number of hats around the school and parish. All her life she'd worked with youth. She gave a common sense answer whether or not her opinion had been asked. This was true even if it did not seem to line up perfectly with the norm of the day, like her steadfast stance supporting Theresa's desire not to get married right away simply because she was pregnant. "Let things sort themselves out and see how it goes," she offered. Sister had a magnetic personality to go along with her good sense of humor. She warned us that after our son's arrival, he would get the wrong impression with a possible avalanche of well-intended gifts (right on), but it was hard to stop a train, and that was what we were facing: a train of folks eager to meet and welcome our new pride and joy. Gradually, we tried to explain to Andrew that every time someone came did not mean a present for him, but he would only break down and cry. He wanted to know why we didn't have two cars like most everyone else on the block. We informed him that we only need one car because Dad did not drive. Several times we attempted to re-immerse Andrew in his Korean culture. We took him to a Korean Catholic Church on Sunday where most of the people were dressed in their Korean garbs for Sunday Mass. He wanted to sit in the back and fought our attempt to introduce him to anyone. Our friend Sheri invited us all over to socialize with her family. On these visits, Andrew made little effort to play with Sheri's two small Korean children. Sheri re-emphasized to us that it may take Andrew a long time to let go of his feelings, and all we could do was be patient and be there for him. In the house across the street from us lived the Sullivan family: Gerri, Joe ("Baldy"), their three boys and their enormous Great Dane, Zimba. They were country folks who delighted in inviting others to join them on their front porch, sip sweet tea, swat some flies and just share small talk. They were the real deal. What we saw is what we got. Baldy was always trotting across the street to unplug a toilet or take a look at the fuse box at our house. He had a knack with kids, wrestling with them in his front yard but not reluctant to scold them for acting up. Many a hot summer afternoon, we'd all pile into Baldy's old pickup, and he'd carry us the short distance down the road to *31 Flavors Ice Cream Store* where he'd treat everyone. Baldy coached little league and patiently taught Andrew the basics of holding a bat and fielding. His mentoring worked wonders and went a long way in getting Andrew to feel comfortable being himself, to not be intimidated by his peers and to trigger his interest in playing sports.

Tammy and Andrew are pictured in
front of the Christopher Columbus statue
at Union Station, our son's first trip
to downtown Washington.

In the spring after Andrew's arrival, Rita found herself increasingly pre-occupied with thoughts of how our son's Korean stepmother back in Pusan might be feeling about her departed child. Rita asked Andrew if he would like to write a letter to his Korean stepmother and share with her how he was doing and tell her about his new family, but Andrew wanted no part of it. So, Rita asked Andrew if it was okay with him if she wrote a letter and sent it. He nodded yes. Rita wrote the letter which F.C.V.N. translated into Korean and forwarded it to Andrew's stepmom. Several months later, we received a letter from one of Andrew's older stepsisters (a Korean version and an English translation). In it, the sister thanked us for writing and told Andrew that his Mom sent him to the orphanage so he could have a chance to come to America and that it was one of the hardest things she ever had to do, but she did it out of her love for him. She closed by asking him to honor his new family and make them proud of him, just as they were proud of him. Over time, things improved, but Andrew continued asking us his blunt questions, often about money. "How much did you pay for me?" He blurted out one evening at the dinner table. As Andrew's English slowly improved, he informed us in broken English that in Korea, they had been told that the streets of America are lined with gold. We shook our heads in dismay. The enormity of what our son was going through became clearer by the day. Before he could reach out and fully embrace his new family, this nine-year-old youngster had to wade through a stormy sea of resentment about his past and the awkwardness of fitting into his new American life.

Despite his lack of proficiency in English, in January 1981, two months after his arrival, we placed Andrew in the fourth grade at Saint Mark's School. It was suggested that osmosis could be the best teacher and being around his peers would benefit Andrew. It worked out well for the most part. Although, one day Rita did receive a phone call from the school that Andrew was "acting up," and she needed to come right away. When she got to the Principal's office, she was informed that Andrew had been giving everybody in his class the finger, and that was totally unacceptable. When all the dust finally settled, it came out that one of his classmates had informed Andrew that "flipping the bird" to someone is like saying "Hello!" And so, Andrew proudly decided to say "Hello!" to everyone around him. Looking back, we all laugh over it, but at the time, it was anything but funny as this was yet another lesson learned by Andrew—the hard way. As an inter-racial family, for the first time we found ourselves occasionally helping our son deal with ethnic slurs. Rita and I would differ on how to handle this. I would suggest the manly, "punch 'em in the nose tactic" while she would offer the more reasonable "walk away" approach. Fortunately, her advice usually prevailed.

Andrew picked up English pretty quickly and within a year or so was speaking remarkably well, but he still had difficulty pronouncing things. One particular ride in the car still brings the whole family to laughter. In the era before seat belts, while driving the kids to school, Rita was startled by a shriek from the back seat. Glancing in the rear view mirror, she spotted Andrew clinging to his partially open door. Easing the car to the curb, she stopped and circled around to a sobbing Andrew. Not knowing any better, he had squeezed the handle of the unlocked door. Hugging her frightened son, Rita patiently explained that he should always be sure the lock button was pushed down and never ever squeeze the door handle. For months afterwards, whenever we were in any car going anywhere, Andrew would caution everyone to "push a button down!"

One year after Andrew's arrival, our entire family was seated in the Prince Georges County MD Courthouse for the final proceedings of our son's adoption. At the conclusion of the brief session, the be-speckled, portly, red-faced judge called Andrew to step up and have a seat in the witness chair. Andrew rose nervously and shuffled over to the stand next to the judge who turned and smiled. He asked our son if he understood what the day's proceedings were all about, and Andrew responded yes. Peeking over the rim of his glasses, the judge inquired, "Andrew, if, at some point in your life, you could do something in return to show your love for your Mom or Dad, what would that be?" Without hesitation, Andrew responded, "I'd give my Dad a cold beer and a cigar!" The somber atmosphere of the courtroom exploded in laughter, followed by applause. Case closed.

As any family who has adopted a child can attest, it is not that much different than raising one's biological child. In either case, there are no guarantees. Bumps in the road and cherished moments come with each. Well-meaning accolades like "That was awful nice of you to adopt" miss the point. In the end, a parent is a parent is a parent.

A short while after the adoption process, one of my managers at the Library thought it would be beneficial for our group to take a public speaking course that included an exercise in extemporaneous speaking. When my turn rolled around, I surprised even myself by sharing our family's adoption experience. Following my speech, I was taken aback when two co-workers approached and asked to speak privately with me. Without realizing it, my presentation had sparked some interest in the adoption process. Over the next several weeks, I met privately with these two different colleagues just as Sheri Simas had met with us. Both families went on to adopt children.

Andrew proudly standing outside the Federal
Courthouse in Baltimore, MD, shortly after the
ceremony inside where he became an official
U.S. Citizen.

On July 2, 1981, Fr. Wells baptizes Andrew at
St. Francis Church in northeast Washington.

In the spring of 1981, Fr. Wells presided with the Bishop at Tammy's eighth grade class Confirmation, and two months later, Fr. Wells was transferred to St. Francis Parish in DC. Earlier, we had asked Fr. Wells if he would baptize our son, not realizing that he would soon be re-assigned. Shortly after leaving, he invited us to his new parish where he conferred the Sacrament of Baptism on Andrew.

Chapter 10

Padre

At Thanksgiving 1981, Fr. Wells invited Rita and me to assist him in conducting a CCD workshop at St. Joseph Mission Church at St. Croix in the U. S. Virgin Islands, which is under the auspices of the Catholic Archdiocese of Washington. A few weeks before departure, Fr. phoned. "I've got some good news and some bad news. What do you want to hear first?" He asked Rita. "The good news," she replied. "The good news," he continued excitedly, "is that I got a hundred bucks off each plane ticket." "And the bad news?" Rita asked. Clearing his throat, Fr. Wells continued, "Well, the bad news is . . . I'm not going!" He went on to inform us that he really needed to stay in the area because of his dad's failing health and this may well be his dad's last Thanksgiving. Fr. Wells then told us not to worry because we would love his replacement, Fr. Bob Amey who had recently been assigned to our St. Mark Parish. The trip was just two weeks away, and we would be spending a week in a rectory on an island a thousand miles away with a priest we hardly knew. We invited Fr. Bob over for dinner, and by the time we finished desert, we'd learned that we shared a lot. He was a classmate of my sister Patty at St. Anthony grade school, and Fr. Bob was a few years ahead of Rita at St. Anthony High School. Having broken the ice, we all looked forward to what would be the first of many trips we would take together.

St. Joseph Mission Church is situated in Frederiksted on St. Croix. Shortly after our arrival, Fr. Bob informed us that he felt comfortable with what many friends at his previous parish called him, Padre, so we called him Padre. At the time of our visit, the sanctuary was a cinder block structure with a corrugated tin roof, glassless windows and no screens. Goats, chickens and lizards wondered about the landscape. Our stay at the rectory included use of the parish car, an old Fiat. The housekeeper was a matronly nun from the Dominican Republic who, among other things, dutifully instructed us to keep the car clean and not to smoke in it. We nodded in humble agreement at her advice as we prepared for our first road trip into town. As Padre carefully backed the car out the narrow driveway with the three of us jammed inside, Sister disappeared behind a small palm tree. Padre and I exchanged glances and smiled as I retrieved two small cigars from my shirt pocket. At the time, we both thoroughly enjoyed our stogies, and now was the time to light up. Of course, we would be sure to leave no evidence behind in the car. We puffed away as we chatted, but during our return trip home, we never noticed how full the ashtray was getting—until the car sputtered to a stop as it ran out of gas. We were a short distance from the rectory when we tried extracting the loaded ashtray from the dashboard; suddenly, it lurched free, sending a cloud of ashes and debris everywhere. The three of us looked at one another and howled like guilty school kids. If Sister caught us now, we were dead meat. We had nothing to clean up the mess with but our bare hands. While Rita and I fruitlessly tried scooping the ashes with our hands, Padre volunteered to go look for some gasoline. A parishioner picked him up, and a few minutes later, he returned with a can of gas. Upon pulling into the rectory driveway, Sister was waiting for us, hands on hips. She inquired about our delay, and peeking inside the car, she discovered our shenanigans. She went to the rectory, returned with a hand vacuum and handed it to Padre, smiling and scolding us at the same time. For the rest of our stay, we had no problem with Sister.

Padre said daily Mass to an eager gathering of barefooted people who literally embraced us each time we were in their company. Everyone wore his/her finest, brightly colored garb for Sunday Mass. Moments prior to the start of Mass, a short parade of dilapidated pickup trucks backed up to the church door where a sea of happy, singing men unloaded a variety of steel drums and carried them to their place inside the church. "Ave Maria" softly played on steel drums was indescribable. Our CCD workshop covered a variety of topics; the children and their teachers seemed to cling to every word we said. We left them with workbooks and pictures of our own class back in the states. During our week with Padre, we discovered the three of us had even more in common: a love for the outdoors, tent camping and a curiosity about places none of us had ever visited. We shared some of our silliness with our new friend, like having fun with the kids by talking backwards and always naming each of our vehicles, including our newly purchased '82 Ford Club Wagon van we dubbed Filmore. The island rectory was actually a small compound where we would sit on the veranda in the evening and be joined by Joe, the resident black lab who'd occasionally leave our company to scamper after an unsuspecting rabbit.

On leaving St. Joseph Mission Church, I only wished that somehow I could have selfishly captured just a few drops of the deep-rooted faith of the congregation, put it in a bottle and brought it back home for a rainy day. The engaging spirit of the Caribbean people was contagious and transcended the daily poverty many of them endure. Our sojourn was a revelation for all of us and drew the three of us back to this part of the world again.

During his assignment to St. Mark Parish from 1981-1984, Padre's influence on our family continued to grow. As time and our schedules permitted, we'd head off for some serious tent camping together, often joined by our friends the Franks and their kids. We had "Hilary," a large family size tent from Sears. Padre had his own comfy one-man pop up. The Deep Creek lake area of Western MD was one of our favorite spots. Filmore was the perfect ride with two large bench seats that could easily come out to store gear for our camping ventures. Occasionally, our kids would bring a friend along or our friends, the Frank family, would join us. Before long, we spread our wings and headed out to distant venues: North Carolina's Grandfather Mountain, Niagara Falls and old Quebec. In the summer of Andrew's senior year in high school, we thoroughly enjoyed our three-week, cross-country camping trek, taking in places like Pike's Peak and National Parks like Rocky Mountain, Zion, the Grand Canyon and Yellowstone. Our outdoor meals were not the traditional hamburger and hot dog variety. Typically, we would stop at a local meat market, and Padre would see to it that we would be treated to a gourmet meal: a slow cooked London broil, a pan of simmering home fries and onions, fresh veggies on the grill and maybe a loaf of fresh baked bread. Everyone had a chore: collecting kindling, setting the table or washing the dishes afterwards. A special highlight of each of these junkets was that Padre always brought along his Mass kit, so if it was a Saturday evening or late Sunday morning, Padre would don his vestments and offer Mass for us around a picnic table. These were pretty special experiences; how many folks ever get to say they have participated in an outside Mass at the North Rim of the Grand Canyon or six miles down a dirt road in the backwoods country of northern Maine? It was not uncommon for neighboring Catholic campers to ask if they could join us in celebrating the Holy Eucharist. It was also a good feeling to have our children share these experiences with us. Our typical camping day would end around a blazing fire. As dusk melted into pitch black, we would huddle around and swap silly (sometimes scary) stories or just listen to the whippoorwills and coyotes serenade us. Occasionally, as the hour grew late and our campfire dwindled to a pile of glowing embers, "Rodney the raccoon" would appear out of nowhere slithering down a tree trunk and sending folks scurrying, signaling it was time to turn in.

While at St. Mark's, Padre agreed to take over as our Couple's Group mentor. His level demeanor and pragmatic approach kept us focused in our sometimes wobbly attempt to stay on track with our faith. As the years ticked by, Padre continued to have a significant influence on our family, even after leaving our parish. With each new assignment, we would pile his belongings into Filmore and help move him to his new parish. Likewise, Padre was always at our side on a moment's call. He was a guiding hand when Andrew got a bad case of high school senioritis, a period in every parent's life when his/her hair turns noticeably gray. Andrew wanted nothing to do with my alma mater, Gonzaga in Downtown DC. He opted to attend our cross-town archrival St. John's where ironically, he thrived in the regimented military school environment. He also enjoyed playing sports, and with good coaches and hard practice, he developed into a pretty decent tennis player. By his senior year, he was the number two man on the high school tennis team, and as a freshman in college, he made the All-Conference Team.

In addition to his friendship, it seems God placed Padre in our life so that the three of us could travel together, and travel we did. Typically, in mid-winter, we would begin making summer vacation plans together. The three of us agreed that our camaraderie led us to visit places we probably would not have gone to on our own. I am sure St. Christopher had a hard time keeping up with us from Key West to British Columbia. Later, we would also enjoy a Caribbean sailing venture meandering the BVIs with my sister Patty, her husband Bill and two other friends, Cely Gregory and Betty Bartholomew. Another opportune trip found the three of us in Munich at Oktoberfest when we were invited to visit old friends Addie and Yuri Azarenko. Taking in the homeland of my great maternal grandparents was pretty special. While in Bavaria, we toured the post card setting of Insbrook. Then heading south, we visited Padua and the Shrine of St. Anthony. In Venice, we somehow survived the two zillion pigeons adorning the plaza at St. Mark's Cathedral and enjoyed the requisite gondola ride with our friends Ben and Anita Lewis (Padre abstained).

Our travels together with Padre are irreplaceable experiences. Together, we witnessed God's handiwork everywhere, in the faces and customs of people, in breath taking landscapes and the obscure resurrection of new life in an edelweiss poking its tiny head through a snow covered slope in the Alps. These experiences could not help but magnify the true enormity and wonder of God's creation. They were also sobering reminders of our own infinitesimal existence not simply in this world, but the cosmos. Traveling with Padre made these experiences even more special. Wherever we were, we celebrated the core belief of our Catholic faith when Padre consecrated the bread and wine into the body and blood of Christ at our daily Mass.

For over thirty years, Padre has been a very special part of our family, celebrating birthdays, anniversaries, family get-togethers and graduations: Tammy's from nursing school and Andrew's from Penn State. He presided at our children's weddings and baptized our grandchildren. He has also consoled us at wakes and presided at funerals of family members and friends.

There is one nagging question I continue to ask my dear friend: "Padre, if we're the same age, how come I look so much older than you?" His response is always the same, a silent, boyish grin.

Pictured (left to right) are me, Rita and Padre (Fr. Bob Amey) during our trip to St. Joseph Catholic Mission Church at St. Croix U.S.V.I. As a mission parish, St. Joseph's is under the auspices of the Archdiocese of Washington.

Chapter 11

The Cross of Love

In late spring of 1985, Nanny suddenly became ill, and on June 17, she passed away. Padre had been at her bedside an hour or so before she died. He had anointed her with the Sacrament of the Sick and said that Nanny was very much at peace. Padre shared with us that in her final moments, Nanny was praying her rosary and told him that she knew it was time to go because she heard a voice calling her. Following Nanny's death, Pop was a wreck. After fifty-six years of marriage to his best friend, he suddenly found himself lost. The unexpected death of Nanny threw all of us into a spin. Nanny had been the outgoing one and Pop the introvert. She handled all the household logistics while Pop busied himself fixing the faucet or resurrecting the garbage disposal. After Nanny's passing, it quickly became evident that Pop was not at ease living alone. Being only three miles away, Rita and I made it a point for one of us to be with Pop daily. After several months of trying to fit this into our daily routine while shuffling two kids to their assorted activities, it soon deteriorated into a hellish mess. It was agreed that the most workable solution would be for us to sell our house and move into Pop's. Our home sold quickly, and we took up residence in our new home, a four-bedroom rambler with a finished basement on a cul-de-sac. The move to the University Park subdivision put me much closer to my carpool, but the next several months were a tumultuous time for everybody. In merging the two households, we went through the arduous task of giving away or selling some of our own furniture. Rita and I set up our living quarters in the basement. Pop kept his bedroom while Tammy and Andrew occupied the two remaining bedrooms on the first floor. Pop's loneliness for his deceased wife manifested itself more and more as he looked to Rita to wait on him as Nanny had done. This included silly things like asking her to change the TV channel for him. The kids would have a few friends over, and Pop grew irritable at the chatter or loud music. This was all so uncharacteristic of him, but he found himself thrust into a new world, and try as we did to make him happy, he was no longer a happy camper in his own home. Pop had no hobbies and was not an avid reader. Since his retirement fifteen years earlier, he had always passed his time contented to be at Nanny's side, be it shopping or watching TV. Rita had gone back to work as a secretary for the Office of Youth Ministry at the Catholic Archdiocese of Washington Center, so Pop spent most of his days alone putt-zing around the house until the kids came home from school. Rita's boss, Msgr. John Enzler, offered Pop a volunteer job in Rita's office a few days a week. Pop accepted but, within a few months, gradually grew less interested and stopped going. His health slowly deteriorated, and he moved slower and slower; eventually, Rita and Donnie convinced him to give up his driver's license. Soon afterwards, Pop's condition reached the point where we could not handle him alone. Despite a consuming feeling of guilt and many sleepless nights, Rita and Donnie came to the same conclusion that their father needed the help of professional caretakers. With the assistance of Msgr. Enzler, we were able to identify a reputable, well-recommended healthcare facility for

Rita's dad. We placed him there, but his stay was short lived. Three weeks later, on October 1, 1986, Pop gave up his spirit and died.

The fourteen-month period caring for Pop was brief, but quite challenging for everyone. None of us anticipated that trying to do the right thing in this situation would wreak such havoc. It had put a strain on our marriage, as Rita felt like a Gumby doll, continually pulled in one way by her dad and in another direction by me and kids. We lost our privacy, I felt like I was losing a wife in the process, and whatever the kids did got on grandpa's nerves. To this day, Rita still has flashes of guilt over the decision to place her father in a nursing home. Although in the end, Rita admitted that placing her father in the hands of professional health care was the right thing to do.

Anyone who has had to care for an aging parent, special needs child or friend will tell you that it can be an all-consuming endeavor. However well-intended, doing more than one is capable of, without admitting outside assistance is needed, can have catastrophic consequences. This brief episode helping Pop was an eye opener for me, changing forever my perception of folks who perform this care as part of their normal day in day routine. How do they do it? Typically, these people carry their crosses with dignity and a smile. One such inspiring person is our dear friend Carol Halderman, Tammy's God Mother, a single mom and widow who is relegated to a wheelchair, yet she goes about each day caring for her forty-three-year-old son and our God Son David, who is also wheelchair bound as a result of being born with Spina Bifida. Over the decades, Carol has been through countless operations and procedures back and forth to various hospitals for both David and herself, but this special lady seeks no sympathy, rarely complains and is usually asking other folks what she can do for them. For as long as I can remember, Carol has been a leader in the Montgomery Co. MD Special Olympics and other service related organizations in her community. My own wobbly attempts at helping others are like grains of sand on the beach compared to the steadfast stewardship performed by personal caregivers like Carol. Whenever I find myself asking, "Why me?", all I really need do is reflect on Carol and my cross suddenly becomes much lighter.

Chapter 12

Making Time for Good Company

Things slowly returned to normal; well, almost. Not long after Pop died, I was hospitalized with a ruptured appendix. My recovery at home lasted a few weeks. During that time alone with our aging, faithful Shih-Tzu, Stinky, I found myself chatting a lot with God, and beginning to dream about retirement. Andy Andrews, Jim Wood, Bill Miller and I worked the "Hotline Desk" at work where we handled technical trouble shooting issues from our end-users. My colleagues visited me at home a few times and on one such trip, they informed me that our team now had a new member, Murph Bader who was joining us from the Copyright automation group.

Since I've never been one to jump out of bed and shoot out the front door if I had someplace to go in the morning, on those days I always gave myself plenty of time after getting up. Shortly after returning to work from my illness, I found myself missing the quiet time I had gotten used to when I was home alone; I needed to continue making time each day for just God and me. So on work days, instead of waking at five fifteen a.m., I started setting the alarm for four forty-five. After showering and dressing, I settled down for the next half hour or so in the comfortable blue armchair in the pre-dawn solitude of our living to say my morning prayers. That was 1986 and the start of my cherished morning chats alone with God. By the time I finished praying each morning, Rita and the sun were both up, and she would have already started getting herself ready for work at the Pastoral Center. We would chat over a few cups of coffee while listening to the old Hardin and Weaver morning radio show, and I would be out the door before six thirty. It was a twenty-minute walk to the home of our carpool driver, Bill Lipford. A bunch of us would board the Brown Jug, an old but reliable Dodge conversion van, that would carry us to Capitol Hill. Our home was in the appropriately named community of University Hills, about a mile from the University of Maryland campus. My morning trek to the carpool in the neighboring area of Lewisdale was the perfect venue for one rosary. Along the way, I enjoyed the cheerful chirping serenade from the birds that were wakening from their slumber. Occasionally, my jaunt would find me whistling back to them one of my favorite tunes, "Morning Has Broken." My walk started with a hefty hike up and down the streets out of our development and ended up having to cross a wide expanse of manicured ball fields. As fate would have it, the middle part of my journey took me along a road through a small patch of parkland woods adjacent to the popular Adelphi area duck pond. This was the scene of an infamous, DC area, unsolved double murder—long forgotten by many that happened back in the mid 50's. It was here that two teenage girls were walking on their way to nearby Northwestern High School when they were ambushed and killed by an assassin's rifle shots. The crime has been referred to as the "Pancho Villa" Murders because supposedly a man was spotted in the area about that time dressed with two ammunition belts crisscrossing his chest. However, no weapon was ever found nor anyone ever arrested. I recall the incident well because at the time we lived about three miles away in northeast DC; I was in eighth or ninth grade, and Dad warned us not to play outside for quite a while. Also, Dad knew one of the victims' fathers who happened to be a police officer in MD. It was a major topic in the news for several weeks. *The Washington Post* has since run at least one anniversary article on this crime several years ago. At any rate, the path I followed twice a day to and from my carpool passed directly by a cherry tree adjacent to a small footbridge that crosses Sligo Creek. It was at the base of that tree where a barrage of spent .22 caliber bullet casings and little other evidence was ever found. Police speculated the killer used the crotch in the tree to rest his weapon, a .22 caliber rifle, while taking aim and firing on his unsuspecting victims nearly a hundred yards away. I'd be lying if I said I didn't sometimes clutch my rosary beads just a bit tighter when I passed by the aging cherry tree: still standing, a mute witness tightly guarding its ghastly secret to that horrific crime those many years ago. One's imagination can easily run wild, especially in the pre-dawn hour of late fall and early winter mornings when the large tree's gangly, leafless limbs, bathed in a clear moonlit sky, cast its lengthy eerie shadow over the creek rushing by below. Just as it was nearly fifty years earlier, that area is pretty quiet that time of day; the only interruption to the stillness might be a welcoming wave from an occasional passing jogger. Every now and then, that friendly smile happened to be Fr. Wells on his morning run, who had been re-assigned to nearby St. Mark's as Pastor.

Each April my evening hike back home from the carpool might catch me stooping to pluck a few dandelions or buttercups from the ball fields I crossed. Since I usually arrived home from work before the little

Mrs., I'd plunk the tiny yellow and white weeds into a shot glass, fill it with tap water and wait for her to come home, usually a few minutes later. When Rita arrived, she would set her purse on the kitchen table, and I would come up behind her and ask her to shut her eyes. Then I'd lift my poor man's bouquet from behind my back and ask her to open her eyes. She'd look flabbergasted and swoon kiddingly, "Oh, you shouldn't have!" Our silly little rite of spring was something we both got a good chuckle over.

Returning to work was good medicine, as was seeing fellow car poolers and co-workers. Catholic colleagues like Mercedes (Mo) Baird, Mary Ann Murray, Mary Donovan and I enjoyed sharing our mutually humorous experiences growing up Catholic. One day a small nun doll showed up atop a nearby cubicle. I think it was Sarah Worcester who claimed credit, but others said that Sister just appeared out of thin air. The lifelike wooden figure in her black and white habit struck a permanent imploring pose, head tilted skyward, hands clasped and pointed to heaven. At her feet rested a small sign, Our Lady of the Perpetual Loop. She may never have helped anyone find that elusive loop while debugging our software, but she always put a smile on our face. Our new colleague in the Hotline was Mary (Murph) Bader who had the unique distinction of being the first female member of our group. Murph patiently put up with our shenanigans and was a perfect fit. A few months after her arrival, Murph's three male co-workers decided it was time to officially welcome her to the Hotline with an appropriate surprise token of our appreciation. When Jim Wood shared his idea and said his wife could help, we jumped on it. Jim's self-deprecating humor always kept things loose. Like the day he abruptly stood up and announced it was time to go home and soak his aching piggies. Stepping from behind his desk, he sheepishly looked down, revealing his unmatched brown and black loafers. When Jim brought in his wife's completed handiwork, we set it on Murph's desk and waited for her return from lunch. Spotting the small, wrapped present and penned note, "Welcome to the Hotline-you earned it," Murph carefully unwrapped the package. Her eyes lit up, and she squealed excitedly as she held up a faux sequin covered jock strap. Murph made no bones about cherishing her unusual trophy and hung it proudly above her desk where it remained until her retirement some twenty years later.

My lunch hour routine could mean a stroll around the U.S. Capitol grounds (before the current jersey wall barricades). At one time, our stroll allowed us to take in the magnificent canopy of giant elms that ringed the landscape of the Capitol before the trees were felled by the dreaded Dutch Elm Disease in the 70's. Lunch also might mean eating a sandwich at my desk before joining my friend Stan Lerner on our usual perch on the low wall on First St. S.E., outside the Library's James Madison Building where we worked. Inevitably, from our low perch, we would sit and solve all of the world's problems and as fate would have it, observe the lunchtime parade of attractive, young, Capitol Hill working women just happening to pass by us each day around that time. Directly across the street was St. Peter's (a.k.a. "St. Pete's"), a venerable large gray stone Catholic Church with tall stained glass windows and a high vaulted ceiling. For me, the pealing of the church bell in the tower simply blended in with the blur of other street noises, except of course on Holydays when the gonging beckoned me and hundreds of other Capitol Hill Catholic workers inside for noontime Mass. One day, while finishing my sandwich at my desk, this crazy notion hit me: why not drop by St. Pete's for the noontime Mass? I caught myself spinning around in my chair to be sure it was not one of my nutty colleagues. A few minutes later, I found myself kneeling in a back pew of the massive church. A minute later, Fr. Michael O'Sullivan appeared from the side sacristy, bowed at the center of the altar, and began to say Mass. Glancing around, I was surprised by the large number of attendees scattered throughout the cavernous sanctuary. Even more surprising was the number of familiar faces. Feeling a bit out of place, I found myself wondering if anyone would recognize me. Just as quickly I scolded myself for even entertaining such a nitwit idea. One of Fr. Wells's familiar cackles came to mind, "Get behind me Satan!" Up until retirement fourteen years later, I traded my noontime perch on the wall, for a perch on a pew, inside St. Pete's.

If I could not make noon Mass and the weather was nice, I would take my sandwich down to the park a few blocks away at 2nd and C Streets S.E., site of the old Providence Hospital. I would plop down on a park bench, eat my sandwich, lean back and relax. Occasionally, I would say my rosary. One such day I will never forget. Having taken the last bite of my liverwurst sandwich, I was leaning forward, elbows on my knees and fingering my rosary when I caught a glimpse of someone approaching from my left. Out of nowhere, a youth appeared in front of me and began leaning hard against my right leg. From behind, someone with his hand on my shoulder barked, "You got any money?" Startled, I looked up and shook my head. Unconvinced, the individual behind me leaned into my ear and whispered, "Dude, maybe you can't hear too well." The youth on my left looked down, spotting my purple rosary dangling between my knees, and asked, "Wait, what's that in his hands, grapes?" Then one of them interrupted, "No, that's one of them rosary things . . . the dude's prayin' or something . . . let's split." Suddenly I was alone again on the bench. The entire episode lasted maybe fifteen seconds but seemed like an hour. A minute or so later, still shaking, I cupped my rosary, slipped it into my pocket, and headed back to work. My head was swimming: what would have happened if I had not brought my rosary (a good chance, absolutely nothing)? Was I spared by some sort of heavenly intervention? Obviously, the one young man recognized the rosary and any lingering respect he had for it caused him to run away from crime. All I know is that the mere sight of my tiny eight-ounce set of rosary beads stopped the Devil dead in his tracks, scattering evil in three directions at once. I do not know if Mary was any more attentive to my intercession to her that day or not. It does not matter whether she was present on the bench next to me or just somewhere in the neighborhood. I am perfectly comfortable believing that our Blessed Mother used this incident to touch the heart of at least one of my would-be robbers and, in a flash, turn him away from this—and perhaps similar, future misdeeds.

The park bench incident convinced me that when we pray in earnest, the individual we are praying to is in fact drawn close to us. I doubt there is any evidence that my attempt to attend weekday Mass and a precious few minutes after Mass all those years, rendered me any holier. However, that period in my life (once again) re-kindled my elusive awareness that if I was serious about having a close relationship with God, just as with anyone else, I needed to separate myself from the clutter of life and spend time together with Him to nurture that bond, not just fit God in with an occasional *Glory Be* or *Our Father* when I really need Him (and then fuming because He didn't always listen). Our faith tells us that ours is not a demanding God, up there impatiently tapping His foot, glancing at His watch, waiting for our undivided, individual attention. He knows better than anyone does how life has a way of derailing our best intentions. Ours is a loving God who seeks our love in return, and He was saddened when I chose not to at least make the effort each day to invite Him into it. It boiled down to a daily commitment that only I could make. I needed to set aside a particular time and place to be in the quiet, good company of Jesus, His Mother, or perhaps to bend the ear of a favorite saint or two. Whenever I manage to follow my own advice, I find them there, waiting patiently for me.

Chapter 13

Hanging the Moon

In the early '90s (then) Speaker of the House Newt Gingrich sponsored an initiative to provide the first public access to all US Congressional legislative activity. The Library of Congress was directed to develop and implement a groundbreaking project that would be rolled out as a web site application on the Internet. Our Information Technology Systems (ITS) Office was tasked to do the job.

The web site to be developed would be titled *THOMAS* to honor Thomas Jefferson, the Library's early visionary who first saw the Library of Congress as a grand public resource for dispensing such information. The internet had been up and running for a number of years, but for many of us, this was our first immersion into developing an internet application. Earlier our Office had provided electronic access to the Congressional Record, Committee Reports, etc. This new undertaking would provide access to legislation (approved and pending) by Bill number, subject and sponsor, lists of sponsors, voting records and such. Soon after the *THOMAS* Team was formed, I was invited to join the group. With my new assignment, once again I was surrounded by very bright and talented minds, engaging characters like Dean Wilder and Susan Thomas who were the real technical brains behind many of the earlier Congressional efforts. In the ever-changing IT world, as always, we spent a lot of time just trying to keep up. Now it meant learning internet display coding such as HTML. A major task in our development efforts involved getting the House and Senate programming staffs to transmit their data to us in a common format. Proving that some things never change, both legislative groups fussed and fumed about any sort of compromise. Each wanted to send their data to us in their own format and leave the figuring out part up to us. Trying to resolve the issue (which we ultimately accomplished) was like trying to get kids to stop their bickering and shake hands. The freethinking spirit of our team kept our supervisor Maryle Ashley more than a little busy. We were often like a clutch of wandering chicks that she was always trying to reign in, but eventually she somehow managed to do just that. Early on, I found myself working with the *THOMAS* homepage layout design group, developing FAQ's. When the curtain came up on *THOMAS*, I was the Dear Abby voice to our end-users via our Email and telephone inquiry lines. Since *THOMAS* was literally open to the world, our clients ran the gambit from an irate staff member across the street upset because the system took more than ten seconds to respond, to a Texas grade school student's inquiry about how to locate her Representative's voting record, or an elderly woman from Boise wanting to know how she could find the status of a particular Medicare bill. While our *THOMAS* team received a number of accolades for completing the task, we also had no problem toasting ourselves at the *Hawk 'n Dove*, a popular Pennsylvania Avenue watering hole.

The winter of '96 was brutal; DC received record snowfall, and everyone was growing weary of shoveling through three-foot drifts. That was when Rita and I decided that come retirement, we were heading south. Both of the kids were married, and we had been enjoying our years of empty nesting. However, a routine colonoscopy on me in February brought another reality check. A golf ball sized tumor was found in my lower colon that was diagnosed as pre-cancerous. I underwent surgery to remove the growth along with about three inches of my colon. The surgeon seemed pleased that they were able to remove everything and informed me I was lucky because another six months and the scenario would have been much different. Everyone was relieved, and I could not help smothering God and my pal Saint Jude with my gratitude. A short time after returning to work, we were all crushed by the passing of our faithful little dog Stinky who lived to be seventeen and hung around long enough to be sure Dad got through his latest healing process okay. In the spring, Rita and I returned, after fifteen years, to the Caribbean; this time it was to the BVI on our much-anticipated sailing venture aboard a sixty-five foot schooner, *Aeolus*. Counting Rita and me, there were seven guests on board: Padre, my sister Patty and her husband Bill, and two other close friends Ceily Gregory and Betty Bartholomew. The ship's crew of two, Mike and Dorothea, doted on our every want for an entire week. This was one of those rare adventures in life where the experience actually exceeded our wildest expectations! It was a true blessing that could not have come at a better time.

Two months after our trip, we headed south with Patty and Bill to investigate New Bern, located near the southeast coast of North Carolina, at the confluence of the Neuse and Trent rivers. A few miles south of town and adjacent to the Croatan National Forest, we discovered a rural community, *The Home Place*. All lots were wooded. We could choose and buy our own lot and pick our own builder. It was an exciting and far different scenario than in the DC area. Rita and I found lot #40, an acre and a half lot with a small stream forming the back property line that separated us from the expansive Croatan National Forest. We plunked down five hundred bucks on the site of our future retirement home, and Patty and Bill did likewise, right across the road from us.

In April 2000, Rita retired from her position as parish secretary for Saint Joseph's Church in Upper Marlboro, MD. On May 3, I retired from the Library. Thanks to our ITS Office Director Herb Becker and the usual detailed collusion of colleagues like Cathy Chou, Ann Christy, and Gail Hitchcock, my sendoff celebration included iced tubs of my favorite Miller Genuine Draft. Thirty-five years in one place conjured up a flood of memories with the usual toasting and good-natured roasting. Colleagues like Lynn Brooks were very much up to the task with quips like, "Contrary to popular rumor, Casem was never originally hired by Thomas Jefferson to clean the horse troughs outside the Library." Near the conclusion of our celebration, I was truly surprised when I was presented one of the highest civilian accolades in Federal Service, the *Superior Service Award*, from the Librarian of Congress, James H. Billington. I accepted the prestigious recognition on behalf of all my talented and unselfish co-workers who over the years always made me look good.

At the beginning of our journey, we were the Flintstones of automation, wrestling with boxes of punched cards containing our software written in a language only a machine could understand. When it was our time slot to "run" our program, we headed to the "machine" (computer) room, balancing plastic canisters of tape housing our precious data. Our computers were gigantic iron monsters that filled entire rooms. They were shrouded in blinking lights and flanked by rows of glass enclosed read/write tape drives, each performing its monotonous chore with whirling and chugging sounds, reminiscent of the wringer washing machine in Grandma's kitchen up in Lancaster. Today's computers slip easily into one's packet. Ours were the Neil Armstrong footprints on the surface of electronic book access. Eventually, we eliminated bibliographic card catalogs forever, and for the first time, it allowed librarians to perform their tasks at the keyboard of computer terminals that were tethered together by jumbles of cables. Now we have the Nook. Our early internet application efforts provided the first public access to federal legislation. Today's iPads and Smart Phones can provide zillions of apps in the palm of the hand, allowing access to global events as they are happening. We did not hang the moon; we just thought we did. Likewise, a few decades from now today's wireless gizmos will be IT relics, stirring fond memories of a bygone era.

Chapter 14

Planting High Cotton

Following our retirements, we had the good fortune of selling our home in one day. We put our furniture in storage with considerable help from my brother-in-law Bill who was in that business. We had already picked a builder for our new home in NC and gave him the thumbs up to start construction. After many light-hearted chats, Rita and I had long since settled on an appropriate name for our new home. We had been planning the details of our new home for a few years. I worked a few extra years to pay off our share of two college tuitions and set some funds aside for our new home. We had also been praying to God, asking if it were His will, our dream would happen. Our new home would be located in Dixie, land of cotton, but a good cotton crop does not just happen. A lot of elements have to fall into place for the farmer: good seed, fertile soil, the right amount of rain, plenty of warm sunny days, and of course no pest invasion. When all things come to fruition, the Lord answers the farmer's prayers—and ours—and we were both blessed with High Cotton!

After selling our house in MD, Rita and I and Hazel, our young shih-Tzu, were invited to stay with our daughter Tammy (and grandson Matt on the way), her husband Jack, little Emily and their boxer Buster in their three story townhouse. It was quite an adventure. While at Tammy's, we attended Sunday Mass at St. Lawrence Church in Odenton. One Sunday, a missionary priest spoke about the plight of children in Central America. After Mass, he distributed some information specifically about the conditions in Guatemala and how to sponsor a child there. We took the literature home, and for the next week or so, when we were able to find some quiet time alone, Rita and I discussed the proposition and prayed over it. We agreed that God had blessed us. In selling our house quickly and being able to save towards our new home, we were in a position to help a child and make a modest financial commitment. We contacted the sponsoring organization the missionary priest had identified, and we received information about several children living in abject poverty. We chose a dark eyed seven-year-old girl named Sonia who lived with her grandparents in a rural village in Guatemala. That was the summer of 2000, and we have been Sonia's sponsoring family ever since. Through the missionary agency, three or four times a year we trade letters with Sonia (hers is accompanied with a broken English translation). Periodically, we receive updated photos of Sonia, sometimes with her family. It's hard to verbalize the feeling we have experienced all these years when this young person, who lives in a region where barely getting by is a way of life, share her joys, struggles and dreams and tell us she prays to God for us every day. Sonia is now in her late teens and looks forward to becoming a secretary someday to help her family out. She recently described how she completed embroidering a tablecloth with fruits and flowers on it and went on to say how much she would like to meet us to give us the tablecloth in person. Having been able to play a small role in nurturing this young girl, and now "watch" her from afar grow into a young woman is so rewarding, but even more humbling. Unwittingly, for all these years, Sonia has showered us with God's love and grace.

Decades earlier, the excruciating heartache of several miscarriages robbed Rita and me of seeing the smiles and hearing the dreams of five of our children. I have little doubt that through Sonia, God allows us a glimpse of those precious lost moments.

Chapter 15

Murder in the Rectory

When the phone rang the morning of June 8, 2000, our world exploded. The call was from Rita's friend Marie to inform us that Fr. (then Msgr.) Wells had been murdered during the night in his rectory at Mother Seton Parish in Germantown, MD. Words cannot describe the gut wrenching anguish that befell all of us. Murdered? How could that be? The sordid, detailed news accounts of this gruesome crime gripped the entire DC area for months. The accused killer, Robert Lucas, was high on drugs, broke into the rectory looking for money and surprised Fr. Wells. Apparently, a horrific struggle ensued before Fr. Wells succumbed to multiple stab wounds from his knife-wielding killer. The much-publicized trial took center spotlight for months; it ended with an outpouring from the Wells family joining thousands of friends in a prayer vigil doing what they knew Msgr. Wells had undoubtedly already done himself—ask for forgiveness for the convicted killer who was eventually convicted of second-degree murder and sentenced to twenty-five years in prison. The stream of traffic stretched miles to Msgr. Wells's funeral at Sacred Heart Church in Bowie, MD, which was his first assignment as associate Pastor. Thousands of folks said farewell to this man who had changed countless lives. Msgr. Wells was laid to rest in the bucolic hilltop setting of the old cemetery adjacent to the original Sacred Heart Church.

Like anyone who ever met Msgr. Wells, even after all these years, it was still hard to imagine never again having the front door burst open and hearing the familiar, "Yoo-hoo! It's me . . . anybody home?" How often did this man take the time to patiently listen to someone's anguished cry to then ever so slowly lift them up and help them put the broken pieces back together again? No doubt, Msgr. Wells busted through the Pearly Gates with that same unassuming proclamation, "Yoo-hoo! It's me . . . anybody home?" If he is not busy praying for each of us, chances are he is greeting Heaven's newest resident. Spotting the familiar face of an old acquaintance, I can almost hear the booming voice down here, "Well, well, well, fancy meeting you here!"

Chapter 16

Earthen Vessels

December 14, 2000 was move in day at *High Cotton*. It was hard to believe, but our dream had finally come to life in rural North Carolina. One of the finishing touches we watched our builder's crew perform was fitting our garage door with a large steel bar. I asked what that was all about, and a burly man wearing a dusty NASCAR cap smiled, "Oh, ah forgot, you're from up north. This here's a hurricane bar for when a hurricane rolls through which means yer house might git blowed away, but yer garage door ain't goin' nowhere."

Welcome to the rural south.

From day one, the honesty, simplicity and hospitality of southern folks touched us. Political correctness does not have much of a chance here. A stranger waving "hey" is not something particularly comfortable in the DC area, and if it happened, instinctively one would grab his/her wallet. The local dialect and relaxed southern pace can take a Yankee some real getting used to. Some never do. *The Sportsman Barber Shop*, where the sign on the front window reads "Open Weds-Fri, 7:30 am—5:30 pm, MORE OR LESS", offers a perfect window into what is important in the coastal, rural south. This one chair operation has been owned and operated for over forty years by my neighbor, Walter (Butch) Cox. There one will likely meet the game warden, a truck driver hauling logs, a handful of local tradesmen or the sheriff passing time waiting his turn in Butch's chair by exchanging opinions on everything from the approaching nor'easter, to the rising cost of farming or those ridiculous rules and regulations from "all 'em folks up there in Washington." Walter's right proud of all the folks who continue to be his customers down through the decades, some traveling forty miles, one-way from Mt. Olive. One day, his sage advice on banking ignited a raucous round of "Amen" when he suggested that the best place to keep money is inside the septic tank, unless of course, it's in the front yard. And, of course, our local weatherman Skip Waters' forecasts would not be complete without tidal information and wave heights twenty miles off shore. Another new experience for us was the Lowe's deliveryman personally calling to apologize for having to re-schedule our delivery for "tomorrow" because one of the youngin's was up all night runnin' a fever. (And "tomorrow" of course did not actually mean the next day, more likely next week or later.) No doubt about it, we had entered a whole different world, and we loved it.

After settling into our new home adjacent to the Croatan National Forest, spring ushered in an awakening menagerie of native crawling, flying and squawking critters. All of them had been life-long residents amidst the swaying Spanish Moss and long needle pines of lot #40, long before we had selected it as the perfect place to build *High Cotton*. Besides deer, much of this wildlife we had never seen up close and personal. Backyard visitors included fire ants, lizards, large red headed woodpeckers, hawks, an occasional black bear or wild turkey. Messy tree frogs, darting geckos and an occasional snake were early curiosity seekers on the front porch. We also quickly realized that the vast wetlands of coastal Carolina are the perfect incubator and major runway for squadrons of mosquitoes. While I have yet to see much proof myself, I am told that the lizards, tree frogs and some snakes eat their body weight each day in skeeters. Oh, and did I mention the humidity? Living near the confluence of the Neuse and Trent rivers and the nearby ocean means come June, a walk out to the mailbox and back and one is soaked, but we quickly discovered the predictable afternoon sea breeze sweeping through the screened porch offered the perfect retreat. At dusk, a whippoorwill's song ushers in an evening medley of croaking frogs and the syncopated "hoot-hoot" of a barred owl. No doubt about it, life at *High Cotton* is galaxies away from the DC beltway and much more than ever dreamed about. Our handful of new neighbors, from the Chudziks next door to the Eddings family up the street, with a friendly "Hey!" all made us welcome.

We enrolled at St. Paul Parish in New Bern where some of our initial acquaintances included Ralph and Joan Limpbach who made us feel right at home. Ralph was a retired Marine who proudly shared his Pearl Harbor experience, and Joan was an avid swimming instructor at the YMCA. One Sunday after Mass, I was approached by Danny Gennantonio who offered me an application to transfer my Knights of Columbus membership into local Council 3303, which I did. In addition to being Past Grand Knight and having worn many official county and state officer hats for the Knights, Danny was the Babe Ruth of recruiting for our Order. The last count was well over four hundred and counting. Many of our council members were also transplanted retirees from the north, and before long, Rita and I found ourselves involved in council activities and surrounded by a whole new circle of K of C families. Who should I meet at a council meeting? Not one, but two fellow Gonzaga Purple Eagle Alums: Jimmy Downs, Class '38 and Jay Mattingly, Class '53. One day I was invited to get my feet wet as a council officer, something I had never had the time or particular interest for previously. However, I decided to give it a try and was elected to the initial chair position, Outside Guard. In succeeding years, I began ascending through the council officer chairs, which meant increasing council responsibilities. Rita and I had also begun volunteering as tutors in the Craven County public school system. We were pretty busy, but we had the time and enjoyed getting back to doing things together. Many of our friends were even busier. The holidays became extra special with visits from Tammy and Andy's families and the grandkids, Katie, Emily and Matt.

As the years ticked by, the more blessed we felt about having realized our dream and making it to *High Cotton*.

In 2004, we attended a workshop conducted by Sister Monique Dissen, IHM, of our St. Paul Church. It was an introductory session to learn about becoming an Extraordinary Minister of Holy Communion (Eucharistic Minister) to the sick in the hospital. While we had previously served as Eucharistic Ministers at Mass, this particular arm of the ministry, which places one among the very sick and dying, necessitates a certain awareness and protocol. Though we were drawn to trying this, we were unsure of whether or not we could actually work in this capacity. That concern was covered in class. Prior to being assigned to this ministry, each candidate accompanied Sister Monique or her assistant Irene Swanteson on several rounds through the hospital. A mutual decision could then be made to proceed or not. Like many others in our ministry class, a strong sense of inadequacy and unworthiness enveloped us. Sister Monique was quite aware of our angst and made no attempt to minimize it. She addressed it, suggesting that such feelings were perfectly normal, and that believe it or not, nearly every saint at some point during his/her life felt the same way. She also pointed out that, aside from the Blessed Mother, there are no perfect saints. Sister Monique concluded by reminding us that we were simply the messengers of God, and that, "We are God's earthen vessels, born to carry His love to one another."

How could we not respond to this call?

For the next several years, every Friday, Rita and I were a team, husband and wife, ministering the Holy Eucharist to Catholic patients at Carolina East Medical Center. As anyone who has served in this ministry can attest, it is impossible to sum up in a few words the special feeling surrounding this ministry.

During the 2007 season of Advent, I was able to share an extraordinary experience with my good friend John Gray. John and his wife, Ann, had recently relocated to New Bern, and John was our Council 3303 Membership Director. He was a Second Degree Knight and very much looked forward to one day becoming a Third Degree. John was also dying of Cancer. He was in and out of the hospital, and when he had completed his chemo treatments, he was sent home. John asked if I would continue bringing communion to him, which I did. Before receiving the Eucharist, John would ask me to join him in spontaneous prayer to God. We would sit side by side on the couch, clasping hands and simply having a conversation with God, as if He was seated in the chair across from us. John's prayers always had a joyful tone, and during our visits together, he would ask me for the names of Brother Knights who were ill, so we could pray for them. Eventually, John became bedridden, and I would sit close to him while he continued to manage a weak smile and reminded me not to miss out on an opportunity to help someone today by fretting over a tomorrow which may never come. He quipped, "Bucket lists are for procrastinators!" A few weeks prior to Christmas, in a now whispered voice, John leaned toward me and asked if I thought there was any way he could receive his Third Degree Exemplification before he died. Trying to hide the crack in my voice, I cleared my throat and assured John I would do what I could to make that happen. Our Order's Third Degree Exemplifications were typically held a handful of times annually across the state at different local councils. The next scheduled Third Degree at our council was not until spring. I was now Deputy Grand Knight of our Council, and I knew a few quick phone calls had to be made very soon. I contacted Mike Durbin, a State officer in Havelock and told him the story. A few days later John Gouldie, our State Deputy (Third Degree CEO, North Carolina Knights of Columbus), phoned to inform me a date had been set to perform the Exemplification, and to get directions to John's house. Before hanging up, John paused and added that Bob Grabowski, our District Master (Fourth Degree CEO, North Carolina Knights of Columbus) would also be there to confer John with our Fourth Degree Exemplification. The Fourth Degree Exemplification represents the highest degree conferred on a member by our Order.

I have a cherished photograph hanging in our dining room of the most memorable day in all my years as a Knight. It is a picture taken following our small, private ceremony in John's home, on Sir John Gray's special day. Several State Officers had stopped everything during the busiest time of the year to drive halfway across the state to make John's dream come true. What better example is there of our Order's principles of unity and fraternity? In the picture, dressed in full regalia, are State Officers John Gouldie, Bob Grabowski and Mike Durbin. Also pictured are members from our Council 3303 and local Fourth Degree Assembly 1820: Sir Knights Danny Gennantonio, Bill Pake, Lud Hartung, Grand Knight Tom Hartman and myself. All of us were gathered around John who was seated, smiling and proudly clutching his Fourth Degree Exemplification Award. To the best of anyone's knowledge at the time, this was the first such occasion, at least in North Carolina, where a dual awarding of Third and Fourth Degrees had ever occurred. My friend John lived to celebrate Christmas with his family, and two days later his suffering was over.

Anyone who has had a similar experience can attest what a humbling honor it can be to be in the presence of a dying person such as John, wracked with the agony of pain, yet somehow managing to exude the joy of an undying faith, knowing he would soon be going Home to his Creator. His earthly journey was ending, and he would soon be at one with his Father. Sister Monique's words rang true, but in a way I never expected. As an earthen vessel himself, John had carried God's love to me.

The following year began one of the busiest twelve-month periods in our married life when I was elected to serve as Grand Knight (GK) of Council 3303. One of the largest councils in the state, with four hundred members, we have a rich history of strong support for St. Paul Church and School as well as serving the many needy in the New Bern community. The thought of trying to do what I could to help continue that tradition was a daunting prospect but something I looked forward to achieving. Surrounded by an excellent slate of officers, I felt comfortable we could make it happen. The annul operation of our council programs involved a myriad of financial fund raising activities and thousands of hours of volunteer service by our members and our wives. Some of our ongoing community support efforts include Right-to-Life programs, such as EPIC (Eastern Pregnancy Information Center), RCS (soup kitchen and homeless shelter), MERCI Clinic, New Bern Senior Center, Special Olympics, our Council's free prescription drug program for qualified indigent persons, Craven County Relay-for-Life Cancer Survivor's team, and LAMB. During this particular year, we were also responsible, along with neighboring councils, to coordinate and host the annual K of C State Convention in New Bern, something that had not occurred here in over thirty years. By year's end, we had also accomplished a milestone in our council's history. We had managed to complete the laborious process of renaming our council in honor of Msgr. James R. Jones, our former Pastor, a strong supporter of Catholic education, and a Fourth Degree Knight who had served as Chaplain at both state and local levels. Thanks to the tireless physical and spiritual support of so many, at the conclusion of our fraternal year, our council was recognized by K of C Supreme Council in New Haven with the *Star Council Award*, which is the highest accolade a local council can receive from Supreme.

In my earlier years as a Knight, someone once quipped that a Grand Knight needed to have three things going for him: a faithful dog, a patient wife and a dependable Deputy Grand Knight (DGK). I was lucky to have all three: Hazel, our faithful shih-Tzu, my bride Rita, and Rich Tomasik, our hard working DGK.

As the year came to a close, I felt my energy sapping. Two years prior to becoming Grand Knight, we learned some very sobering news about my deteriorating health and a condition we had hoped would never become a reality.

Chapter 17

The Party's Over

In February 2006, Rita and I had our usual back-to-back appointments with our family physician, Dr. Ken Wilkins. When it was my turn for him to review with me my annual test results, Doc gave me the somber news that my kidney function was significantly below normal. Numb and silently hysterical, I sat there in silence. Dr. Wilkins assured me there was a lot that could be done to treat this condition, and he would be referring me to a Nephrologist, Dr. Richard Blair who specialized in kidney disease. My mouth suddenly felt like sand paper, and I felt a knot tightening in my stomach. Getting into the car, Rita asked how things went, and in a sobbing voice, I blurted out the news. We wound up driving over to St. Paul's where we parked the car, held each other for a long time in silence and both cried. The familiar words to the country song Don Meredith used to croon many moons ago on Monday Night Football darted through my mind. "Turn out the lights, the party's over . . ." Finally turning to each other again, in a whispered voice, Rita assured me everything would be okay. Wiping away our tears, we made a brief visit to church. Returning to the car, we did what we always did in troubled times.

We said the Rosary.

Our initial visit with Dr. Blair lasted a long time. He performed some preliminary testing which confirmed that I was suffering from Chronic Kidney Disease (CKD), or kidney failure. He shared a wealth of information about the illness and pointed us to several resources which we could use to begin educating ourselves about CKD, including United Organ Sharing Organization (UNOS), the official keepers of the kidney transplant waiting list for the government. I told Dr. Blair of my history of kidney issues at birth, where it seemed that one of my kidneys was doing most of the work. Over the next few months, Dr. Blair initiated a battery of renal tests. The results confirmed that I was in Stage 3 (moderate) CKD. My diagnosis indicated that my CKD had stemmed from my condition at birth and as such was labeled as being Congenital. Other tests showed my left kidney had atrophied and was now barely working at all while my right kidney had grown to the size of a small football because it had been doing most of the work for over sixty years and was now wearing out. The protein output level in my urine was 1,000 times above normal, which meant my kidney filtering system was just about useless. Many of the chemical levels in my body were also out of whack due to my kidney failure. My total kidney function was around 24%. Dr. Blair informed us that while kidney disease could not be reversed, with proper treatment, it could hopefully be stabilized for an unknown period of time. The first level of treatment appropriate for this stage of CKD was prescription drugs which I began that were specific to my needs. My new daily regimentation included a re-focused prayer life. Since I was losing my kidney function, I began asking St. Anthony (Patron of folks looking for lost things) to help me deal with my situation. Sts. Jude and Patrick were already in the arena. Also, I made a concerted effort to be extra vigilant about keeping the rest of me as healthy as possible. I resumed my modest one-mile daily walk and continued meeting regularly with Dr. Lois Flemming, my chiropractor, who worked to keep my back and the rest of me upright and moving. I kept Stroud Tilley, my pharmacist, busy filling my grocery list of meds, and I listened to his sage advice. I even quit dragging my feet about getting some needed dental work done and gave Dr. Donald Whitley the green light to have at it. Rita and I continued our appointments with Dr. Blair, who monitored my condition and adjusted my meds as needed. Although my ongoing diagnosis over the next four years reflected a gradual decline in kidney function, I was able to maintain a relatively normal pace. However, eventually my energy level noticeably declined, and despite adjustments to meds, I began retaining more fluid and found myself fielding more comments about my ashen color. Although I'd ratcheted up my spiritual plea bargaining, my trepidation about what lay ahead persisted.

Little did I know, but my anxiety was about to mushroom from a sucker punch life was about to deliver from an entirely different direction.

Chapter 18

Once a Parent

Any time we're around our K of C friends, sooner or later, laughter will fill the air. The 2010 New Year's Eve party at our K of C Council Hall was no exception. For us, that was brought to an excruciating end with the ringing of Rita's cell phone. It was Tammy's husband Jack who was informing us that Tammy had been admitted to the hospital suffering from what was believed to be an overdose of some kind of medication.

About two years earlier, Tammy and her family had relocated to New Bern. Their marriage had been unsteady for a few years, but with two children, they hung in there. Recently things had continued to deteriorate, and Tammy and her husband separated. Tammy was living at their house with the children. We had been observing the situation for quite a while. When Tammy asked for assistance, we tried to do what we could as parents and grandparents. As her dad, I could not help but notice over the past few years that my daughter's eighteen years of nursing were taking a physical and mental toll on her. Like many young girls, Tammy had always wanted to be a nurse, and she never waivered from her goal. From the start of her career, her firey, Irish heritage kept her passionate about treating each patient professionally without foregoing compassion. She was never bashful about what type of patients she wanted to serve: the critically ill and the dying. Her assignments included the E.R., shock trauma, dialysis and hospice. One of her shock-trauma patients was mortally wounded Prince Georges County, MD Police Officer Sgt. John Novabilski. She received several outstanding reviews, but in the fall of 2009, for the first time in her career, Tammy resigned from her job. Soon after that she began treatment for substance abuse. Throw in a failing marriage, and on New Year's Eve 2010, it all came crashing down. She hit rock bottom.

Following her divorce, Tammy retained custody of the children. With dwindling resources and battling a nightmarish illness alone, it was not pretty watching what was happening. We made the only choice we could as parents. We had to save our 41-year-old child. We invited her and our grandchildren, Emily and Matt, along with Gus, their boxer, into our home. They joined us and venerable shih-tzu Hazel, and, just like that, *High Cotton* became home to three adults, two kids and two dogs each wrestling in his or her own way with both grandpa's and Tammy's situations. In early March 2010, Tammy faced up to fact that she needed to pull out all the stops to treat her illness, and she agreed to undergo rehab for substance addiction. We sent her to a rehabilitation facility in MD. When she returned from rehab, we were pleasantly shocked by the changed person we saw; there was a hint of the old Tammy with a glimmer in her eye and a new attitude toward her condition. The grandkids, who had been very much tuned into mommy's scary moments, could see the difference too. However, all of us knew that rehab was not the end; it was just the beginning of a one-day-at-a-time challenge for her. Tammy resumed counseling and began faithfully attending her various support sessions. We introduced her to Deacon Dr. Mike Mahoney, a staff member at our St. Paul Church. Tammy began regular counseling sessions with Deacon Mike, and over a period of several weeks, we could see an even greater awakening in our daughter's spiritual focus and self-esteem. Between her regular support meetings and her sessions with Deacon Mike, Tammy slowly began the arduous journey of picking up the pieces and starting over. Rita and I began attending ALANON meetings, a support group for anyone affected by a family member or friend suffering from alcohol addiction. We spent our 45th anniversary with Tammy at one of her open support group meetings where I stood up and tearfully thanked the roomful of strangers, battling the same demons as our daughter, for all their love and strength they had already provided Tammy.

With school buses coming and going, impromptu off key mini concerts by aspiring young musicians, an occasional Sponge Bob bullet in the back, or a sneak attack from a plastic helicopter hidden in a couch cushion, *High Cotton* was no longer an old folks home. It often felt like all of us were being engulfed by some kind of tsunami. A quiet place or privacy became elusive commodities. I became increasingly angry with God. Life had been turned upside down, again. Finally, one evening, I made myself a resolution to get back to my old prayer life and find a quiet place for some mediation. I retreated to the bedroom, shut the door and headed for my chair. No sooner had I sat down than from the kitchen came raised voices over homework, serenaded by two barking dogs. My silent ranting with God erupted again, "Please give each of us the strength to get through this! What happened to that thing about never giving anyone any more than they can handle? You know our bucket's full . . . talk to me!" Closing my eyes, I leaned back and somehow managed to doze off. The next thing I knew, half-an-hour had passed. I sat up and did something I never do. I randomly flipped open the Bible and began reading in the middle of a page. My heart jumped. It was Psalm 145:2:

"The Lord supports all who are falling
And raises up all who are bowed down."

Then the lightbulb came on. Tammy and I were both facing our own day-to-day struggle to survive that which would continue for a lifetime. We were each on our own battlefield, fighting our own relentless foe, but despite our broken condition, we could be there for the other to lean on. A while later, I came across a spiritual intercessor I could have used forty years earlier. In my newly rejuvenated roles as dad and grandpa, he was a perfect fit: St. Joseph, Guardian of the Holy Family. I welcomed St. Joseph under the Big Top, cautioning him that we were not such a holy family at that very moment, but we were working on it.

Tammy successfully continued moving forward in her recovery. Her commitment more than inspired me. She blamed no one for her disease. She admits who she is and tries to take care of herself today because tomorrow will come soon enough. Her faith in God has grown as well. Through the unselfish and caring spirit of her alcoholic and addict support groups, she has surrounded herself with folks who admit their own shortcomings yet steadfastly refuse to wallow in self-pity. It is so much more than just attending meetings. It's about dropping everything at any moment to go help a fellow alcoholic or addict who is about to or already has fallen short.

Personally, I see a strong parallel between the tenets of these anonymous, non-denominational recovery support groups and the Christian journey. Each day, folks in these groups make a commitment to get themselves through just that day and any other person who needs help to get through that day. They also admit they cannot do this alone. They acknowledge a higher power (whatever one chooses to call his/her god) and admit that they need to draw strength from that power. The recovery process also involves each individual making his/her painful way through a series of prescribed steps to remaining sober or clean and then beginning again, one step at a time.

Chapter 19

Blue Devils in White Coats

On our February 2010 visit with Dr. Blair to review the results of my latest round of tests, he revealed the news we had been dreading to hear. My current diagnosis indicated my total kidney function had slipped to below 30%, and I was approaching Stage 5, End-Stage Renal Disease (ESRD). Although we had read the literature, like every other CKD patient, we hoped this day would never come. Hearing the words "End-Stage" shot a numbing wave of terror over me. How long before I die? For the next few weeks, Dr. Blair met several times with us, patiently answering our questions and concerns while focusing on options that I would be facing in the near future. He provided even more detailed information about my choices. The direction we chose to follow was up to us, but he assured us that he would try to answer any concerns and support us in whatever we chose to do. Essentially, a person in end-stage is faced with three options: do nothing, dialysis, or get a kidney transplant. Mindful that there were no cures for kidney disease, only treatments, I was consumed with anxiety about learning as much as we could about what was on the table. As I would soon learn, some treatments were better than others. The amount of available information was more than a little overwhelming. There was so much to absorb, so many rocks to look under. We read and re-read literature, visited and re-visited websites. Soon all the charts and graphs ran together, but we pushed on.

Listening to the personal experiences of kidney transplant recipients trumped the ocean of technical jargon. Transplant patients like my cousin Donnie Leppley and friends Billy Lamb and Ann Kwasnick (a double organ, kidney and pancreas transplant survivor who also went through Duke) all shared their journeys.

The following is a snapshot of what all we digested about end-stage options and what eventually led me to the path I chose.

—Do nothing: For religious reasons, some people refuse dialysis. For personal reasons, others choose not to go through the ongoing rigors of dialysis and its typical debilitating side effects. For persons suffering from a major secondary illness (e.g. stage 4 Cancer, serious heart/lung/liver problems, etc.), dialysis may not be an option. Also for the quite elderly, dialysis may not be recommended. Since dialysis can leave a person with an overall weakened state, kidney transplant recipients who have not been on dialysis fare much better than former dialysis patients. Postponing dialysis or choosing to do nothing usually results in the end-stage patient dying within two to three years.

—Dialysis: Relatively speaking, it is a good treatment for kidney disease. It involves a mechanical replication of the kidney function. The efficacy of this treatment is influenced by the person's overall health. Once placed on dialysis, any remaining kidney function ceases, and barring a kidney transplant, the patient remains on dialysis for the rest of his/her life. A fistula is a surgically established interface that allows the patient's blood supply to be cleansed and flushed through a dialysis machine. At any given time, there are over 300,000 people on dialysis

—Get a kidney transplant: A transplanted kidney can come from a deceased donor or a living donor. Receiving a deceased donor kidney is certainly a better treatment for kidney disease than dialysis. A myriad of factors determine the life of any transplanted kidney. Statistics show life expectancy from a deceased donor normally range from a few years up to ten or so years, but many survive significantly longer. Though a more difficult path, receiving a living donor kidney is the best treatment of all for kidney disease. Because the donor has been screened and the transfer time of the kidney is minimal, statistics indicate life expectancy of a living donor kidney is eight-to-10 years longer than that of a deceased donor kidney.

In either option, the person needing a new kidney must first qualify as an eligible kidney transplant recipient. This screening process is conducted at a kidney transplant center where the candidate undergoes extensive physiological and physical examinations and testing to determine his/her eligibility to receive a kidney transplant. This can be a lengthy process, taking up to several months. Screening looks at things like health history, current overall health condition and testing for hidden and potentially dangerous viruses. Adverse findings in any of these areas could eliminate a candidate from becoming eligible to receive a kidney transplant. In addition, a candidate seeking a new kidney identifies a caregiver. The caregiver is responsible for the needs of the kidney transplant patient before, during and following any kidney transplant operation. This includes assistance at home, items such as personal needs, transportation and financial record keeping. The caregiver is also responsible for getting the patient to and from the transplant center for all scheduled appointments. In addition to the actual transplant surgery, this typically involves several pre-op and post-op appointments. For that reason, the caregiver is also screened regarding his/her overall health and to ensure awareness of the time commitment involved.

There are over 220 kidney transplant centers in the U.S. with several in North Carolina, including Duke University Medical Center, a leading research hospital ranking in the top tier nationwide. In selecting a center, one important factor to keep in mind is distance, as multiple trips to the center will be necessary, often requiring the additional cost of overnight lodging. Once a person is placed on the kidney transplant waiting list, expected wait time can range anywhere between two-to-seven years. At any given time, there are 90,000 persons are on the waiting list. Annually, about 4,500 of them will receive a kidney transplant, and 30% of these will be from a living donor. As of 2011, every four hours, someone dies waiting for a kidney.

Because of patient privacy laws, no doctor or medical facility can speak on behalf of a person seeking his/ her own live donor. That person must be his/her own advocate. A potential kidney donor must also undergo extensive screening similar to his/her loved one who is waiting for a kidney.

Traditionally, only one of five potential living kidney donors qualify as a matching donor for his/her loved one. Exciting new concepts paired with rapidly changing technology are greatly increasing the availability of living donor kidneys. The Paired Kidney Donation Program allows one qualified but unmatched recipient/donor pair to agree to be placed on a database to possibly meet and swap with another pair that matches their criteria.

Another emerging source for a living kidney donation is Altruistic Kidney Donation. As the name implies, here a person who is willing and qualified essentially makes his/her kidney available via a database for anyone in need with matching criteria. Emerging options such as these proliferates the miraculous blessing of strangers helping strangers!

End-stage renal treatments are extremely expensive. Annual dialysis cost per patient can easily approach $250,000. Total kidney transplantation costs (pre-transplant screening, surgery and post op) can be upwards of $300,000. Ongoing post-transplant, anti-immune medications and any other required prescription drugs for a kidney transplant recipient can approach $2,000 per month. The present level of Medicare partnership with end-stage renal treatment makes these treatments viable options. Persons in end-stage kidney failure can be eligible for Medicare coverage. Private insurance and available financial assistance programs can certainly further reduce out-of-pocket costs for a given patient. However, the reality is that without the current level of coverage provided by Medicare in this arena, few, if any, persons suffering with end-stage kidney failure could afford any of these life saving treatments.

After digesting as much information as we could, I informed Dr. Blair of my three-pronged plan. In light of its chronic debilitating side effects, I wanted to postpone dialysis for as long as possible while pursuing a living kidney donor and trying to get placed on the transplant waiting list. He suggested I consider preparing myself for dialysis, should I get to the point where I need to initiate treatment by having a fistula procedure. A fistula involves minor surgery, usually in the upper arm, where a vein is reset in a manner to serve as the interface port with a dialysis machine. Normally, it requires six weeks or so after surgery before the fistula is "seeded" and ready for use. An optional and much less desirable temporary dialysis interface is a catheter fistula. This involves invasive surgery where a catheter is inserted through a hole in the chest cavity, and the catheter becomes the dialysis interface. This option invites significant infection and is typically used only in emergency situations. I agreed to have an upper arm fistula procedure, and in late April 2010, Dr. Michael Hallagan, vascular surgeon, performed the successful procedure at CarolinaEast Medical Center in New Bern.

We discussed transplant centers with Dr. Blair. We had Duke in mind but wanted to get his input. I asked him if he was recommending a transplant center to a family member, which would it be? Without hesitation, he said "Duke." Just as quickly, I blurted, "Then Duke it is!" He said he would forward a recommendation to the Kidney Transplant Program at Duke Medical Center. Having lived across the street from the University of Maryland campus for many years, the impish ten-year-old boy inside me could not resist my parting comment, "Geez doc, I never thought one day I'd be putting my life in the hands of the Blue Devils!" Rita shot me her familiar glance before turning to exchange polite smiles with Dr. Blair.

In mid-August 2010, Rita and I made our first trip to Durham, home of the Duke University Blue Devils. There we sat around a conference room table at Duke Medical Center along with five other candidate/caregiver pairs to begin our intake session with the kidney transplant program. In front of us was a stack of documents. The all-day venue conducted by Carolyn Boone, MSN, was comprehensive and detailed, covering everything from pre-transplant screening and testing, the transplant operation itself, post-transplant monitoring, to the ongoing anti-immune medications the transplant patient would require. She also discussed the possible short and long term debilitating and potentially lethal side effects associated with some of these meds. The most sobering presentation addressed the extremely costly aspects of a kidney transplant, including Medicare, other medical insurance and financial assistance options.

At the conclusion of the intake session's general presentations, candidate/caregivers who remained were invited to meet with the pre-transplant team. Our pre-transplant team consisted of the team leader (Leslie Hicks, MSN), the patient (me), caregiver (Rita), Nephrologist (Dr. Matthew Ellis), my surgeon (Dr. Kadiayla Ravindra), a psychiatrist/social worker, a dietician, and a financial rep. Over the next few hours, each team member interviewed us privately, detailing his/her role in the process and gleaning appropriate information from me and Rita. This comprehensive evaluation included current health, medical history, psychological and lifestyle review, and financial situation regarding medical coverage. A collective determination was then made regarding my eligibility into the transplant program. On August 13, 2010, I received my acceptance letter from Duke along with my Duke MRN#. I was officially in the hands of the Blue Devils in white coats.

Our first trip through the halls of Duke Med in September was an abrupt introduction into a very special place: our new world of hope. Making our way toward our initial screening appointment, we found ourselves joining a grotesque procession of pathetic souls in search of their own miracles: a woman shuffling along bent over at a ninety degree angle, tethered to an i.v., a man in a wheelchair without any limbs, a gurney carefully being wheeled by masked attendants, carrying their precious passenger, bandaged from head to toe like some sort of mummy. Accompanying each of these were the personal caregivers, unsung heroes clutching appointment schedules, water bottles and cloth sacks jammed with medications, test kits, crackers and cell phones. They were but travelers alongside their loved ones on the crowded path to hope. On our drive back to New Bern following that first appointment, I was consumed with the realization that compared to the sea of humanity in search of healing, my own pain was perhaps a ripple. A line from Charles Dickens's tale, *A Christmas Carol*, came to mind, "Regardless (of our human condition), we are all fellow passengers to the grave . . ."

Shortly after starting my screening process, I began the awkward endeavor of seeking my own live donor, triggering a lengthy emotional and spiritual roller coaster ride. I was overwhelmed by the number of family and friends who offered to donate a kidney for me and all of the folks who told me I was in their prayers. My spirits soared. Counting family members and friends, no less than eight individuals contacted Duke and began the extremely rigid kidney donor screening process. These special people included several Brother Knights and their spouses. Countless others were praying, but as time went by, our jubilation fizzled as one by one, for a variety of reasons, my potential donors were eliminated. By late November, the last of my eight donors had been disqualified. My heart sank, and I had no answer to my own question, who's left to ask? Opting to postpone dialysis as long as possible, hopefully receiving a new kidney first, I realized I had only so long to accomplish my plan. If statistics meant anything, I became increasingly haunted by the fact that without dialysis, sixteen or so months remained on my expected survival clock.

Chapter 20

Friends in Higher Places

 F unny how when one senses the Grim Reaper has just turned down his/her street, the mind becomes crowded with nutty thoughts of all the woulda, coulda, shoulda's of life. The Devil has a field day watching us squirm and moan with anxiety and guilt, or at least he was with me. One morning, my spiritual focus took an abrupt U-turn. Ever since my list of possible donors had vaporized, my stomach stayed in a knot. While lying in bed and staring up at the ceiling that particular day, I began to accept the possibility that God just might have His own plan for me (as He usually does). A small voice whispered that it was time for a reality check. We knew from the outset that getting a matching donor was somewhat of a long shot. So what if I wound up on dialysis? I would be at the same level of treatment as legions of my fellow end-stage patients already were. Meanwhile, I was still in the pipeline for getting qualified to receive a kidney via the waiting list. I figured that with Heaven besieged with all the prayers and best wishes on my behalf and me being in excellent hands at Duke, what more could I really expect? It was time to let go. I began praying for the sea of folks much sicker than I, all the other persons needing a kidney more than I, and especially those who would never live to see their dream come true. I asked God to forgive my selfishness and implored my pal St. Jude to be sure to move all those people ahead of me in the line for his healing intercession. I would wait my turn, even if it did not come. In the process of making this spiritual U-turn, I found myself including other folks who needed prayers but whom I never had prayed for before, like all the bothersome and irritable people around me. I began praying for each of them by name, asking God to soften their hearts. Pretty soon I found myself acknowledging my own growing impatience and cynicism, so I asked God to include me in the list of irritating people and to please help me soften my own heart. During this time of turning my prayer outward, I gradually began to feel an overbearing weight being lifted from my shoulders. My haunting anxiety over my kidney situation melted into a peaceful, almost joyful resignation to leave whatever grandiose plan there was for me in God's hands.

In early February 2011, our phone rang. Rita answered. On the other end was the unexpected, familiar, exuberant voice of Theresa, the young girl we had invited to live with our family thirty-two years earlier. Wow! What a surprise! After leaving our home with Jonathan, Theresa married Jonathan's dad, Jeff Palumbo. They had three more sons and life became very fast paced. All four sons graduated from college, and Jonathan earned his MBA. We had not gotten together with Theresa and Jeff in decades, but we kept in touch by exchanging notes in Christmas cards. In our 2010 Christmas card, Rita informed Theresa of my kidney situation. Rita handed the receiver to me, "Here, it's for you," she smiled. I immediately recognized the bubbly voice on the other end, but before I could say anything, Theresa proclaimed, "I am so sorry to hear about your illness . . . you know what, I want to try and help you!" I could not believe what I was hearing, nor could I stop the tears that were suddenly streaming down my face. In our ensuing conversation, Theresa told me that she had recently informed God in her prayers that since her life had kind of settled down for a while, she was ready for her next big challenge. In her typical, giggly manner, Theresa announced to me, "I'm positive you're it!" The next several minutes were very emotional for me, Theresa and Rita. Fr. Wells's declaration three decades earlier about us taking Theresa into our home suddenly came barging back into my mind, "I promise, you will never regret this!" I asked Theresa if she happened to recall Fr. Wells words, and without hesitation she said, "I sure do!" The three of us began laughing and agreed that this phone call proved the "Wellser" was still very much up there working on us! I babbled to Theresa and Rita that something pretty special was going on here. This was like "God's Circe of Grace," we all agreed. I told Theresa I would be putting the packet of kidney donor information from Duke in the mail the next day. After hanging up the phone, my mind continued to race. How could this be happening to me? What did I do to deserve this? Rita and I sat on the couch, held each other tightly and cried like babies. Finally, taking a deep breath, we wiped away the tears and began reminiscing about how we first encountered Theresa. Before long, we were hugging each other and crying again.

My own transplant screening continued with regular three hundred mile round trips to and from Duke. Tammy often went along with us and asked questions that we would have never thought to ask. She became like a guardian angel to both Rita and me during the entire process. My sister Patty also helped with the driving. At Duke, I was turned upside down, inside out, checked and re-checked for existing physical ailments, hidden viruses and anything that would preclude me from receiving a new kidney or even tolerating the five-to-six hour kidney transplant operation. The ordeal seemed to drag on beyond what we had expected, but throughout the process, we were always treated in a professional and compassionate manner. Team Leader Leslie Hicks was very understanding about our frustration and emphasized again that the cautious pace was for my benefit. It was better to identify something sooner than later. She was the hands-on anchor to our swaying ship of anxiousness. Meanwhile, Theresa had begun preliminary screening but informed Duke she had to postpone the full battery of exams until June because was a school teacher. Near the end of my testing in late March, concern was raised about a possible condition with the right chamber of my heart. A normal catheter procedure to investigate the heart was not feasible because the fluid used for the procedure would shut down my existing kidney function, and I would have to be placed on dialysis. Heart Specialist Dr. Terry Fortin performed a dry catheterization procedure. The results showed no malfunction in the chamber, and my screening process was finally over. Dr. Ravindra, my surgeon, reviewed my transplant profile and informed us that my expected wait time on the waiting list would be five-to-seven years.

The week following our conversation with Dr. Ravindra, we received devastating news that Rita's brother Donnie, who had been diagnosed with Cancer just six months earlier, was now at home in hospice care. Rita, Tammy and I quickly packed a few things and headed for Bowie, MD. Walking into Donnie and Sue's home on that occasion stopped me dead in my tracks. I hardly recognized him, sitting in his favorite chair, wrapped in a blanket, leaning forward, gaunt and wracked with pain. Donnie's familiar snow white hair was now slightly messed and thinned from the chemo.

When he saw us come into the room, Donnie looked up and smiled weakly. He told Tammy how glad he was that she could come because he needed her help. Donnie's hospice nurse was very comforting and professional. Tammy introduced herself and informed the woman that she was a former nurse and had worked in hospice. Sue invited Tammy to spend the evenings with her and Donnie, which she did. Along with his family, we were blessed to have the opportunity to spend a few moments alone with Donnie the evening before he passed away. Our friend Padre (now Msgr. Bob Amey), who knew the Harners well, presided at Donnie's Memorial Service. Before heading back to North Carolina, an old friend, Terri Stark, handed me a small, faded, holy card with an abstract of a bearded monk. As it turns out, it was St. Benedict (namesake of Pope Benedict XVI). On the back of the tiny card was the story of this fabled sixth century saint who not only founded the Benedictine Order, but is also Patron of persons suffering from kidney disease. I did not think they even knew about kidney disease back then, but apparently Benedict earned his title by surviving an ill-advised attempt by some disturbed, fellow monks to poison his kidneys. Terri thought I might want to include this ancient prelate to my pool of heavenly intercessors, which I certainly did.

Two weeks after returning home, on May 12, 2011, we received the great news we had been hoping and praying for. I had been placed on the kidney transplant waiting list! In June, Theresa's kidney donor screening process resumed, and she began inching her way through the myriad of rigid exams. A lot of folks everywhere picked up the pace of their prayers. Near the end of the month, Deacon Mike hosted a Healing Service at Christ

Episcopal Church in New Bern. Rita, Tammy and I attended. There I prayed for my brother Tommy and asked God if it was His will, let Theresa and I be a match.

On July 29, our phone rang. It was Theresa calling on her way home from Duke. She had just met with her transplant team, and they informed her that our DNAs indicated we were a "perfect match." As a matter of fact, she said excitedly, "They indicated they rarely see matches like ours unless it's parent/child or sibling/sibling!" The team asked Theresa if we are related, and she said no but went on to tell them the story of how we met. When she finished, all they could do was shake their heads in wonderment and surmise, "You all must have friends in higher places!" Theresa assured them, "Oh yes, we sure do!" While her DNA markers testing was complete, Theresa had to undergo the remaining gambit of kidney donor screening.

In September, our son Andrew invited us to join him on a getaway to Cancun. The timing could not have been better. After getting the thumbs up from my transplant coordinator, I packed my meds, promised to be careful and we took off for a week of relaxing and re-couping in the sun. We also thoroughly enjoyed the dolphins swimming right outside our balcony.

Meanwhile, Theresa's trek through Duke continued for an excruciatingly long period, full of stops and starts. As frustrated as we were all becoming, our respective transplant teams including my new team coordinator Venessa Neal, MSN continued to patiently remind us not to be overly concerned; there were no red flags, and the meticulous pace reflected Duke's top priority: the ultimate long-term health of each of us after transplantation.

Finally, in mid-January 2012, we got the word. We were good to go. Our dual transplant surgeries were scheduled for Duke University Hospital Monday, February 6, 2012. I was giddy with delight, and I had to tell the whole world. Well, not quite, but I did send off several rambling vollies proclaiming our pending miracle, emails to family and friends, to Oregon, New York and points south. I also took the time to mail a handful of old fashioned letters of our good news to several individuals who had been part of our journey. Two of these persons I had never met. One was Sonia, our sponsored child (now a teenager) in Guatemala. The other was Ken Sowers, CEO, Duke University Hospital. The postman also delivered my brief epistle to several clergy who had provided encouragement and guidance to Rita and me along the way.

Rev. Msgr. Mike Wilson, Pastor, Our Lady Star of the Sea, Solomons, MD—(Then) Fr. Mike was Theresa's parish priest who guided her as a teen and who introduced her to our family.

Rev. Msgr. John Enzler, CEO, Catholic Charities, Archdiocese of Washington—(Then) Fr. Enzler was Rita's immediate boss as Director of the Office of Youth Ministry at the Archdiocese of Washington Pastoral Center. Msgr. Enzler was also a wonderful family friend and advisor when we were struggling with the failing health of Rita's dad.

Most Rev. William Lori, (then Bishop of Bridgeport, currently Archbishop of Baltimore) and Knights of Columbus Supreme Chaplain—Coincidentally our current Supreme Chaplain had touched our lives many years earlier. Rita had occasions to work with Bishop Lori when they were both at the Pastoral Center. Through Bishop Lori's kind efforts, we met Mother Teresa at the Shrine of the Immaculate Conception in Washington.

Most Rev. Michael Burbidge, Bishop of Raleigh—As our diocesan Bishop, we had met Bishop Burbidge during his many visits to our St. Paul Parish in New Bern.

The kind tone of the replies from these individuals thanked me for sharing our amazing story and hoped it would help someone else's journey. The most endearing response came from Sonia. In a broken English translation of her letter, she wrote, "After reading the letter I pray every night before going to sleep, when I get up and sometimes when I am in the school. I want to tell you that I ask God that you improve your health soon because God listens to us. That is why I trust in Him because he is father to each of us as human beings."

Pictured (left to right) are Andrew, Rita, me and
Tammy at our home on Christmas 2011, six weeks
before my kidney transplant.

Chapter 21

Lifted up by Prayer

In the days and weeks prior to our scheduled surgery, countless emails, Mass cards and simple best wishes notes poured into our home. Some came from folks I did not even know. From our St. Paul Parish, Fr. Paul Mizner, Deacon Mike and Sister Monique prayed privately over me. I was overcome and numb with joy. The family could only smile and watch as Grandpa occasionally wandered about the house, tearfully mumbling, "We have so many good friends" or "What a beautiful day it is!" The day prior to leaving for our surgery in Durham, Msgr. Gerald Lewis and Fr. Vic Gournas jointly anointed me with the Sacrament of the Sick.

On Monday, February 6, at o' dark hundred, Rita, Tammy and I arrived at Duke University Hospital (DUH). Andrew and some friends were already there, as were Theresa's husband Jeff and a few of their sons. By 7:30, my surgeon Dr. Ravindra had visited me in pre-op. I informed him that I was praying really hard for him, as were an awful lot of other people. He looked me in the eye, squeezed my hand and thanked me. He smiled and said he would do his very best for me and assured me everything would be fine. By design, Theresa had arrived half an hour before me. She was across the room from me behind another curtain. I could not miss her giggling exchange with her own team. As scheduled, Theresa preceded me into the O.R. where her surgeon, Dr. Terry Brennan, led her surgery team performing one final careful examination of her kidneys to ensure there would be no surprises and to make one final confirmation which of Theresa's kidneys they would remove. Once my team got the green light, my final prep was completed, and at 9:25, I was wheeled into the O.R. adjoining Theresa's O.R. Five hours later, Theresa and I were in ICU Recovery. Both patients were doing quite well, and Theresa's transplanted kidney was chugging away just fine inside me.

Few people in my life have reflected Christ's Unconditional Love for me more than Theresa Palumbo. Through the boundless prayers of so many people and Theresa's extraordinary decision to literally give part of herself to me, God unfolded a miracle and saved my life.

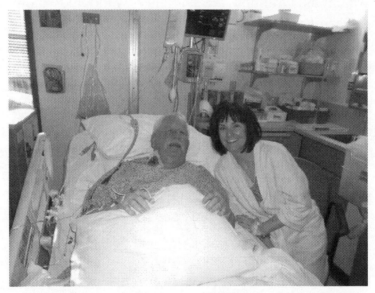

The day following our dual transplantation surgeries
at Duke University Hospital, Theresa visits me in ICU-Recovery.

Theresa was released from the hospital two days after surgery while I remained six days. We were both required to stay in the Durham area for post-op monitoring. Both of our families were staying at the same facility, Duke

Towers Residence. It was pretty neat being able to visit and relax. During these visits, Theresa and I shared about what all had happened. We agreed that that day's events were just as much spiritual as physical experiences. During our own pre-op procedures, each of us could feel the strength of all the prayers and good thoughts entering every pore of our body and giving us strength for what was about to happen. The spiritual rain was continuing to descend on us from near and far: prayers of family and friends from New Bern to Oregon and everywhere in between, several parishes, two Bishops, Theresa's middle school students, our K of C families, the Sunday School class at Tabernacle Baptist Church in New Bern, and our sponsored child Sonia's prayers from Guatemala. All of that did not even count our angelic cheerleaders upstairs, folks like Fr. Wells and the zillion other saints we had enlisted for the cause. What a spiritual army! As Theresa and I were being wheeled out of pre-op, each of us clearly felt ourselves being lifted up and carefully carried by Our Heavenly Father through the skilled hands of our respective surgical teams into the O.R. where God unfolded His miracle.

A week and a half following surgery, I was allowed to go home. My strength was slowly returning, and I had resumed walking and was up to a quarter of a mile a day. It took quite some time, but I eventually settled into my daily regimentation of taking my anti-immune and assorted other prescribed drugs three times a day as directed. For the rest of my life, my anti-immune drugs are required to wage their daily battle against the natural instincts of my body to reject Theresa's kidney, which was not there when I was born. As we learned back in orientation, long-term use of these high risk medications are known to cause diseases like diabetes, stroke and Cancer. With a depressed immune system, one becomes more vulnerable to minor infections and ailments. Back and forth, this war continues every day inside every kidney transplant recipient, but this ongoing, daily regimentation and vigilance is a very small price to pay for having a new life! For the initial few months, we also had to closely monitor vital signs, insulin levels, liquid input/output and weight. We were also returning to Duke every other week for follow up labs and consultations. It seemed like each day I could feel my energy strength inching upward. By four months, I was back up to a mile a day. I must have looked pretty raggedy prior to surgery because now everyone was telling me how good my color was. My meds continued to be adjusted as needed, and ever so slowly, life was getting back to normal. Duke was very pleased with my progress, as were we. Theresa was also doing quite well and had returned to her teaching job a month or so after going home. Today, I feel re-born and consider February 6 as my second birthday. I found myself counting the days out of surgery, telling anyone I met precisely how old I was. "Today I'm . . . days old!" The sixth day of each month marks another month of my new life.

As a kidney transplant recipient at Duke, my 24/7 post-transplant coordinators are folks like Joanne Prinzhorn, RN and Judy Smith, MSN. Regardless of the situation, concern or wherever one may be, this staff always responds promptly in a professional, caring manner.

When a person receives a donor kidney, he/she also gets the urethra that comes with the new kidney. The urethra is the membrane-like tube that connects the kidney to the bladder. One of the procedures associated with most kidney transplant surgeries involves inserting a temporary stint inside the new urethra. The stint aids the urethra in performing its function until it becomes acclimated to its new environment. Typically, within a few months following the transplant surgery, the stint is removed. At the end of March, we returned to Duke to have my stint removed.

We were about to learn a lethal intruder had already taken up residence near my new kidney.

Chapter 22

Agony in the Garden

Urologist Dr. Michael Fernandino carefully examined the inside of my bladder with the miniature camera before removing the stint from my urethra while Rita sat across from the large color monitor watching the procedure. I declined Dr. Fernandino's invitation to watch, choosing instead to lie there with my eyes closed, silently mumbling a bunch of *Hail Marys*. I could hear Dr. Fernandino's verbal description to his nurse and the rest of us of what he was observing, when abruptly he became silent. He suggested that I might want to see something. I opened my eyes and leaned toward the monitor. Another quiet pause and Dr. Fernandino began again. "This is normal . . . this is fine . . . but see this?" Pointing to the wall of my bladder and what resembled a miniscule upside down jellyfish with tiny tentacles extending upward, he observed, "This is not normal. We have a problem here. This is Cancer."

I was dreaming. I knew I must have been having a nightmare. This doctor was telling someone he had Cancer . . . poor soul. Rita returned my look in startled silence. My heart was thumping. My mind was alternately numb and spinning. Other people get Cancer, not me. Dr. Fernandino removed the stint and cautioned us that he would not know for certain that it was Cancer until a complete biopsy of the tumor was performed, as well as the bladder lining, bladder wall and surrounding area outside the bladder. Dr. Fernandino said he hoped he was wrong, but he had performed enough of these exams to feel more than a little certain that this was an early growth Cancer. He also indicated that in light of my kidney transplant condition and ongoing anti-immune medications, any necessary Cancer treatments would, of course, have to be closely coordinated with Dr. Ellis and my transplant team. I had had no signs of trouble, no indication of anything like this going on in my bladder and later learned that it was because it was a very early form of the disease. After checking out of the examination area, we picked a bench in the hallway where Rita sat close to me. We held hands, and in between sobs and strange periods of silence, we mouthed the words to each other everything would be fine. I could not stop wondering the significance of all we had gone through. Did poor Theresa give up her kidney for nothing? No one wants to hear the C word, but I remained optimistic and was thankful at least they had found my Cancer and at an early stage. That would not have happened unless I'd had the transplant, and that would not have happened without Theresa. Before returning to our hotel, we were notified of the pre-op date for the biopsy procedure and exam, which would be performed in the hospital. We remained in Durham until pre-op was done. During this period, I found myself pondering the hidden concern on Dr. Fernandino's face when he candidly informed me I had Cancer. Poor fellow, I thought, how many times has he had to tell a patient that? Then I thought back to Dr. Wilkins's look when I first learned my kidneys were failing and then Dr. Blair's awkward expression when he told me I was in end-stage. How easy it is to forget that physicians, nurses and techs are all human too. How often do they go through the unpleasant task of having to tell a patient or his/her family the bad news, all the while maintaining a composed countenance? How it must weigh on them. From that point on, my prayers included the doctors and all the medical folks who were looking after me.

The day prior to returning to the hospital for my biopsy procedure and examination, we stayed at our usual favorite spot, Duke Tower Residence. It was a warm April afternoon as we strolled around the interior courtyard garden area. There we parked ourselves on a shaded bench beneath an arbor cascading with Confederate Jazzman. We had brought our books along, but we took our seat and sat there silently watching some small children playing nearby. It was Tuesday of Holy Week. I could feel a lump forming in my throat as I pondered what tomorrow would bring. I thought of the first decade of the Sorrowful Mysteries, two thousand years ago and the aguish Jesus must have felt in the Garden that night, knowing what horrific events awaited Him the next day. Whatever bad news I might be facing would be microscopic in comparison to His fate. I thanked Him again for dying for me and asked Him to give me the strength to do whatever I needed to do. I nudged Rita and asked her if she remembered this was the beginning of Holy Week. Her eyes glistened as she nodded and squeezed my hand. Then we did what we always do.

We said the rosary.

The following afternoon, April 4, 2012, Dr. Fernandino met privately with Rita and Tammy in a consultation room on the surgery floor at Duke Hospital. My biopsy procedure and local exam had been completed in the O.R. Dr. Fernandino was smiling broadly. "Mr. Casem did quite well," he informed them. The tumor was easily removed, and there was no sign of Cancer at that time in the bladder lining or wall and no apparent penetration into other areas. A few days later, the biopsy report confirmed Dr. Fernandino's findings. There were no remaining signs of Cancer, and no treatments would be needed at that time. For the foreseeable future, I will be scheduled for regular screenings at the Duke Cancer Center. God's Providence can certainly work in ways far beyond our comprehension. Had my bladder Cancer appeared prior to my scheduled kidney transplant surgery, the surgery would probably never have taken place. However, with my kidney transplant and requisite post-op procedures, the newly arrived Cancer was discovered and successfully removed. Through Theresa's incredible act of kindness, God spared my life not once, but twice.

Chapter 23

The Transfiguration

"**Y**ou've got to be kidding!" shouted Fr. Vic when I told him it was my six-month anniversary since receiving Theresa's kidney. That day was also August 6, Feast of the Transfiguration. "This ain't no co-inky dinky," I assured him. He grinned and pumped my hand. For the next few moments, Fr. Vic shared stories of special events in his own life or others' that occurred on special days. No doubt about it. God has a way of reminding us, "Hey, today's a big day, for me and for you!"

I am blessed to have lived comfortably and, together with Rita, to have been able to make a difference in the lives of Theresa and Jonathan. I am also blessed to have been afflicted and broken. Through the power of prayer and Theresa's unconditional love, God raised me up and made me whole again. A year and a half after receiving Theresa's kidney and since then becoming a Cancer Survivor, I am more than upright and walking. I am transfigured. That is to say that God has unequivocally unveiled His loving presence in me and in those around me. I liken my exhilaration today to another character from my favorite Dickens's tale, *A Christmas Carol*, Ebenezer Scrooge. After encountering the Three Spirits of Christmas (past, present and future) in a dream on Christmas Eve, Ebenezer awakens and finds himself a new person, giddy with delight, never again wanting to be his former self. Acknowledging the true meaning of Christmas, why we celebrate it and who we celebrate it for, he is eager to begin giving and receiving freely, appreciating what he has and never again wanting to skirt by the marginalized person in front of him on the sidewalk because he makes him feel uncomfortable.

There are nearly 200,000 Mikies walking around today, alive because each of them has received someone else's kidney that is now working inside him/her. A third of these persons have received a kidney from a living donor, an unconditional gift of love from his/her own Theresa. I have already felt the hopeful spirit from the multitude of my brother and sister Cancer Survivors. All of these, and other afflicted individuals, have their own stories of incredible journeys and their own miracles.

The path to healing is crowded with weary travelers. Each day many of them heave a sigh of relief to see a familiar figure standing by the roadside. It is Christ. He greets them by name, and just as He has promised all faithful sojourners, He whispers, "Come with me this day and rest in my Kingdom forever."

Chapter 24

Infinite Possibilities Born of Faith

Our universal Roman Catholic Church celebrates this 2012-2013 YEAR OF FAITH by reminding us to choose God by serving others. What a wonderful personification of this spirit we have in the recent election of Cardinal Archbishop Jorge Bergoglia of Buenos Aires, Argentina as the new Pope Francis, Holy Father and global leader of our Church. Our new Pope's own life of humility as Cardinal and Archbishop has very much mirrored the life of the saint whose name he has chosen for his papal title: St. Francis of Assisi. A revered thirteenth century saint, Francis of Assisi was the son of a wealthy Italian merchant. Inspired by Jesus' gospel messages to travel lightly and serve the needy, St. Francis chose to live simply and in poverty among those he served where he washed the feet of the afflicted, fed the hungry and consoled sinners. St. Francis of Assisi is often quoted as having said, "Preach the gospel at all times, and when necessary use words." Aside from routine acts of kindness, the call to preach the gospel can come crashing into our laps out of nowhere or perhaps through the vague awareness of a stranger somewhere facing a crisis. Preaching the gospel through actions can sometimes demand an extraordinary response on our part. All persons of faith have received the gift to do extraordinary things. Sometimes we are the giver and sometimes the recipient. To open ourselves up to such acts, all we need to do is trust in God, let go of our fears and follow our heart. Our heart is the engine of our human existence. We may or may not like what our heart is telling us to do, but it cannot deceive us because our heart and soul are the center of our being and connect us to God, who is the Source of Truth. Therefore, when my heart or "gut feeling" or "that little voice inside" speaks to me, I am hearing the voice of God, my Creator. I should listen closely. He just might be inviting me to experience His Circle of Grace, where He can reveal to me the unimaginable gift of discovering His particular love for me and why He gave me life on earth here and now.

Theresa concludes the story of our journey by sharing her joy when she did just that.

"It is an indescribable gift to catch a glimpse of God's purpose for your life. Both Jonathan and I know the joy of that gift. Without Mike and Rita's generous, open hearts, our paths might have been very different. I am so very grateful to God for the blessing of the second family I 'accidentally' found. A friend asked me after the surgery if I felt scared beforehand. I can honestly say that I was not. Despite months of testing obstacles, I knew that I was meant to be Mike's donor. I had complete peace about our doctors, the procedure and the outcome. I am certain many of my loved ones had serious concerns, but outwardly, they were nothing short of wonderfully supportive. The prayers of many were answered on February 6, 2012.

"The following prayer from St. Therese de Lisieux perfectly captures what I have learned during our incredible thirty-two year journey.

'May today there be peace within. May you trust God that you are exactly where you are meant to be. May you not forget the infinite possibilities that are born of faith.

May you use these gifts that you have received, and pass on the love that has been given to you. May you be content knowing you are a child of God. Let this presence settle into your bones, and allow your soul the freedom to sing, dance, praise and love. It is there for each and every one of us.'

"I was blessed beyond measure by the opportunity to be Mike's donor. I still marvel at the idea that a part of me is inside him. But then again, he and Rita have been a very important part of me for many, many years."

About the Author

M aurice Patrick (Mikie) Casem was born in 1942, in Washington, DC, where he attended Gonzaga High School. In 1965, he graduated from Wheeling Jesuit University, Wheeling, WV with a degree in English Literature and married Rita Harner. In 2000, Mikie retired from the Library of Congress after 35 years as a technical writer and software developer. Rita retired from the Archdiocese of Washington as a parish secretary, and they relocated to New Bern, NC. In Washington, they volunteered for seventeen years as CCD Catechists and served as a speaker couple with the Archdiocesan Pre-Cana Program. They are currently parishioners at St. Paul Catholic Church in New Bern where they have served for a number of years as Extraordinary Ministers of Holy Communion (Eucharistic Ministers) to the sick at the hospital. The couple has also volunteered as student tutors with the Craven County Public School System. Mikie has been an active member with the Knights of Columbus since 1971. He is Past Grand Knight of Council 3303 and a member of the Fourth Degree Assembly 1820 Color Corps. In 2005, the Casems were recognized by Council 3303 as Knights of Columbus Family of the Year. They have two children, Tammy and Andrew, and three grandchildren, Emily, Matthew, and Katie. Mikie is also a freelance writer.

References and Resources

Saint Joseph Edition of the *New American Bible*

His Way by Fr. David Knight

Mere Christianity by C.S. Lewis

A Christmas Carol by Charles Dickens

Library of Congress: visit www.loc.gov

Library of Congress THOMAS, in the spirit of Thomas Jefferson, legislative information from the Library of Congress: visit www.thomas.gov

Archdiocese of Washington: visit www.adw.org

Diocese of Raleigh: visit www.dioceseofraleigh.org

Knights of Columbus:

K of C Supreme Council, New Haven, CN: visit www. kofc.org

K of C North Carolina State Council: visit www.kofcnc.org

K of C Msgr. James R. Jones Council 3303, New Bern, NC: visit www.kofcnewbern.org

K of C Prince Georges Council 2809, College Park, MD: visit www.kofc2809.org

Note: A wealth of current information about Kidney Failure is available on the internet. Listed below are many of the sites I found most helpful during my own research.

American Association of Kidney Patients: visit www. aakp.org

American Kidney Fund: visit www.akfinc.org

The Coalition on Donation: visit www.shareyourlife.org

Forum of ESRD Networks: visit www.esrdnetworks.org

Centers for Medicare & Medicaid Services: visit www.medicare.gov

National Kidney Foundation (NKF): visit www.kidney.org

National Kidney & Urology Diseases info Clearinghouse: visit www.niddk.nih.gov/health/kidney/nkudic.htm

Transplant Recipients International Organization (TRIO): visit www.trioweb.org

United Network for Organ Sharing (UNOS): visit www.unos.org

Transplant Centers—National Kidney Registry (NKR): visit www.kidneyregistry.org

Centers for Disease Control (CDC): visit www.cdc.gov

CarolinaEast Medical Center—New Bern, NC: visit www.carolinaeasthealth.com

Duke University Medical Center: Kidney Transplantation www.dukehealth.org/services/transplants/about www.nephrology.medicine.duke.edu./faculty www.dukehealth.org

www.urology.surgery.duke.edu

Duke Transplant Services Report (pdf)—Duke Services